Chart Topping Drum Beats 1

By Nate Brown

The 60s through Today

Get the accompanying video course by Nate Brown
onlinedrummer.com/chart-topping-drum-beats/

Copyright © 2014 by OnlineDrummer.com
All Rights Reserved.
ISBN-10: 0-9895-8702-9
ISBN-13: 978-0-9895870-2-0

OnlineDrummer.com
PO Box 351
Madison, OH 44057

About The Author

Nate Brown received his bachelor's degree in education from John Carroll University in Cleveland, OH and has over 18 years of teaching experience.

Nate authored the Alfred Publishing's 2013 book *Alfred's Beginning Workbook For Snare Drum,* the feature article for Drum! Magazine, *Dr. Fill: A Step-By-Step Approach To Unleashing Your Creative Fill Potential*, and a number of ebook releases by OnlineDrummer.com: *Take Control Of Your Accents, The Rock Shuffle, 108 Ways To Leave Your Paradiddle, Ostinato Threes,* and *I Ain't Afraid of No Ghost.*

Along with writing, Nate is a well-established video clinician, running three monthly video lesson series including Drum! Magazine's *Groove Analysis Lesson Series*, OnlineDrummer.com's *Monday Lesson Series*, and Jammit.com's *Tuesday Lesson Series*. He also appeared in the DVD *Drumming For Fanatics* by Drum! Magazine and Alfred Publishing and performed at the San Jose Drum! Night 2012. Nate's video lessons have received over 10,000,000 views to date.

Using his successful teaching philosophy, Nate holds private lessons with students from all over the world via Skype. Nate puts a strong emphasis on foundational coordination building as well as making sure students understand when, where, why, and how these foundational techniques have been used throughout the years. Students are motivated by learning songs that incorporate the foundational material being learned.

Nate is also publisher of the popular educational website, OnlineDrummer.com. This site has earned multiple honors under his leadership including being recommended in the book Drums For Dummies (2nd edition), 2014 Best Website Runner-up Drum! Magazine Poll, and being touted in the London Metro as, "The ideal place to find out about drumming." Nate's vision for OnlineDrummer.com is to bring drumming education by talented teachers to everyone with the desire to learn.

Nate started playing music at age 3 but is a strong believer that it's never too late to start. He has seen success stories over and over again of people starting an instrument later in life. If you're hesitant to start because you think it's too late, Nate will be the first one to tell you to pick up the drum sticks and play. It can change your life.

Website: OnlineDrummer.com
YouTube: YouTube.com/onlinedrummer
Facebook: Facebook.com/onlinedrummer

Table of Contents

LESSON 1: GETTING STARTED...4
    INTRODUCTION..5
    LEARNING TECHNIQUES..6
    OTHER CONSIDERATIONS...9

LESSON 2: 8th BEAT..10
    INTRO TO 8th BEAT..11
    8th BEAT COORDINATION BUILDING...12
    8th BEAT CHART-TOPPERS..15
    COMPOSITION EXERCISES..23

LESSON 3: SNARE MOVEMENT..24
    INTRO TO SNARE MOVEMENT..25
    SNARE MOVEMENT COORDINATION BUILDING..26
    SNARE MOVEMENT CHART-TOPPERS...31
    COMPOSITION EXERCISES..36

LESSON 4: 16th NOTE BASS PHRASING..37
    INTRO TO 16th NOTE BASS PHRASING..38
    16th NOTE BASS PHRASING COORDINATION BUILDING...................................39
    16th NOTE BASS PHRASING CHART-TOPPERS..42
    COMPOSITION EXERCISES..48

LESSON 5: 16th NOTE SNARE PHRASING..49
    INTRO TO 16th NOTE SNARE PHRASING..50
    16th NOTE SNARE PHRASING COORDINATION BUILDING.................................51
    16th NOTE SNARE PHRASING CHART-TOPPERS..58
    COMPOSITION..62

LESSON 6: EMBELLISHING..63
    INTRO TO EMBELLISHING..64
    EMBELLISHING COORDINATION BUILDING...65
    EMBELLISHING CHART-TOPPERS..73
    COMPOSITION..80

Lesson 1

Getting Started

INTRODUCTION

LESSON 1 — GETTING STARTED

This book explores the foundational techniques of playing drum set, including tips, tricks and real-world examples of how the techniques are used in chart-topping songs. An emphasis is put on conveying the importance of learning the material you're learning. Knowing the reason you're practicing certain techniques is a motivation. Upon completion of this book, you will have mastered the foundational drum set techniques that have driven song after song to the top of the charts.

Why Learn to Read Drum Set Notation?

Many drummers shrug off the idea that it might be important to learn to read music. Simply stated, it is important! Because you're able to read the English language, you're able to follow along and learn by reading this book. Similarly, reading music is a learning and sharing tool. It's another way to express your art and to access others'.

The Notation Key or Legend

Drum set notation is unique in that there isn't a standard method that everyone agrees upon for notating the drums. Because of this, all drum set notation should include a *notation key*. If no key is present, it's up to the drummer to make an educated guess. Below is the notation key that we'll use for this book.

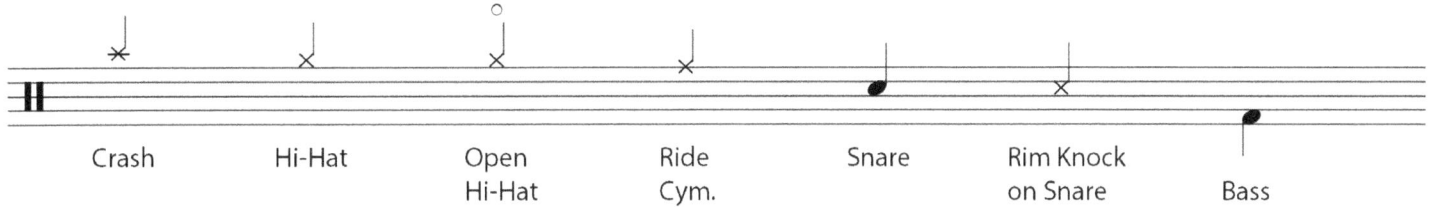

The Mother Of All Rock Beats

Quite possibly the most played drum beat of all time, the groove below is about as basic as it gets. It's actually difficult to go through an entire day without hearing this beat at least once. Many chart-topping songs have used this groove all the way to the top of the charts. *Back in Black*—AC/DC (1980), *Enter Sandman*—Metallica (1991), *Rocket Man*—Elton John (1972), *December*—Collective Soul (1994) and even *Baby One More Time*—Britney Spears (1999) are just a few examples driven by this groove.

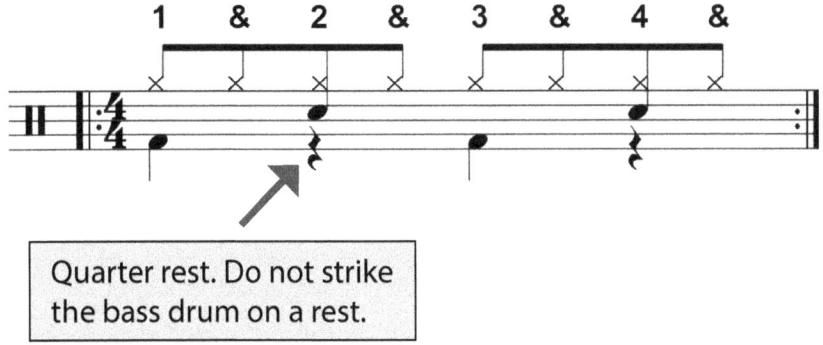

Quarter rest. Do not strike the bass drum on a rest.

Before attempting to learn this beat, read the next few pages which explain common learning techniques and explore other helpful topics to make your learning process more successful and efficient.

Chart-Topping Drum Beats 1 – *The 60s Through Today*

LEARNING TECHNIQUES

Discovering Your Learning Style
Every drummer has a learning style that works best for him/her. What works for another drummer might not work for you. It's important to explore different learning techniques until you find a method that's best for you. Consider the following learning techniques. You may even find that a combination of techniques is the key to your success.

Learning A Drum Beat With The "Vertical" Technique
When learning a new beat, I find that the "vertical" approach to learning the beat helps my body become comfortable with the groove quickly, and I also find it easier to comprehend the groove this way.

With the vertical technique, play the beat count by count, playing all the drums that line up *vertically* on each count. With this method you can play any beat, even though you might be playing it very slowly at first.

The example below outlines how to learn the "Mother Of All Rock Beats" from page 5 using the vertical technique.

On count "1" play the **hi-hat** and **bass** together.

On count "&" play the **hi-hat**.

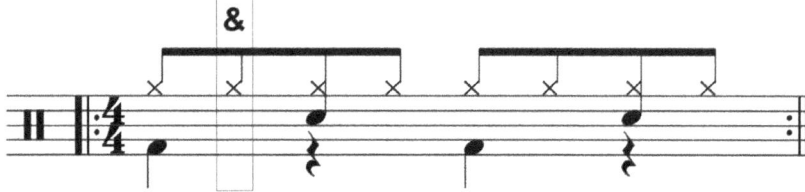

On count "2" play the **hi-hat** and **snare drum**.

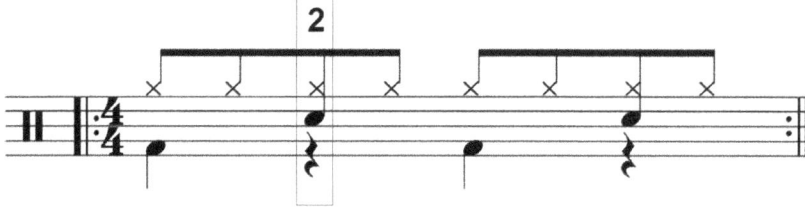

And so on...

Start very slowly, making sure to keep consistent timing. As your body becomes comfortable with the groove, gradually increase the speed. Eventually, you'll have it nailed.

Chart-Topping Drum Beats 1 – *The 60s Through Today*

LEARNING TECHNIQUES (cont.)

Learning A Drum Beat With The "Limb by Limb" Technique

Some drummers prefer to learn a beat by mastering each limb separately, and then putting all the limbs together to create the full groove. The example below outlines how to learn "The Mother Of All Rock Beats" from page 5 using the limb by limb technique. You may choose to learn the limbs in a different order than presented, but for the sake of this example, we'll start with the hi-hat.

Firstly, learn the hi-hat limb. Practice until you're very comfortable with the part.

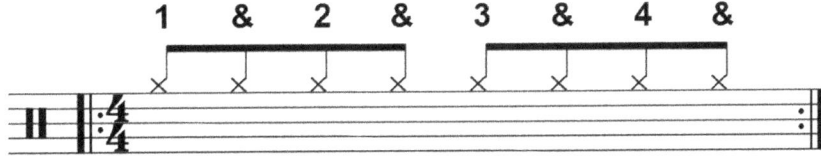

Secondly, learn the snare drum limb, again practicing until you can play it comfortably.

Thirdly, learn the bass drum limb.

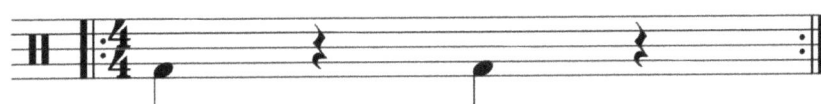

At times, you might find it beneficial to learn the hands' parts together before playing the full groove.

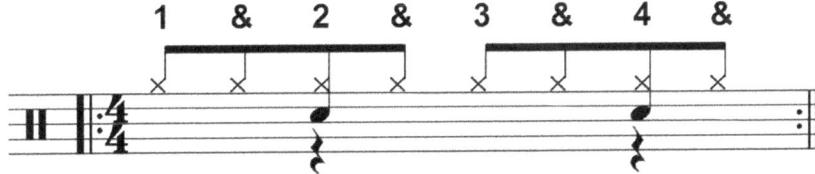

Finally, put all the limbs together to create the full groove.

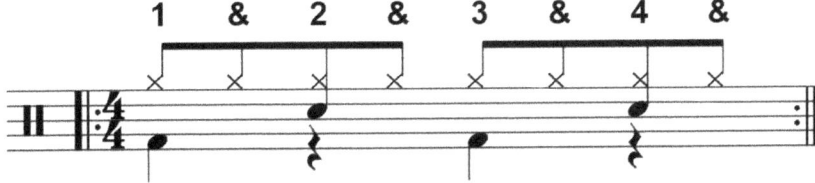

Whether the limb by limb technique is your preferred choice or not, it's good to keep it in your back pocket. This technique might come in handy with a pesky groove down the road.

LEARNING TECHNIQUES (cont.)

LESSON 1 — GETTING STARTED

Learning A Drum Beat In Small Chunks

Chunking a drum beat into small parts is often helpful when learning a new groove. With this technique, you first learn all the strokes in beat 1. Once you're comfortable with them, learn the strokes in beat 2. Then, play beats 1 and 2 together. Keep progressing through the groove this way until you've learned it.

See the example below demonstrating how to learn the "Mother Of All Rock Beats" from page 5 by chunking.

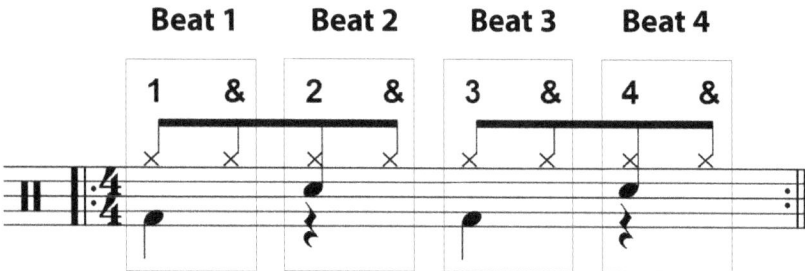

Firstly, practice beat 1. Play it until you're very comfortable with it.

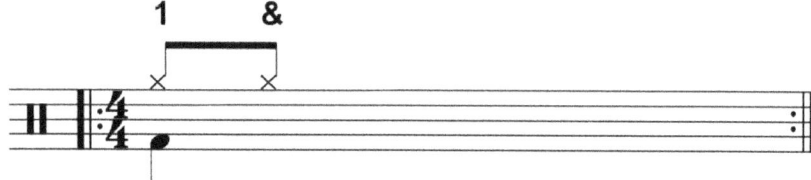

Secondly, practice beat 2 until you're comfortable with it.

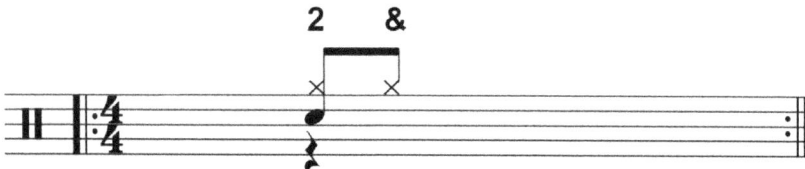

Now add both beats 1 and beats 2 together.

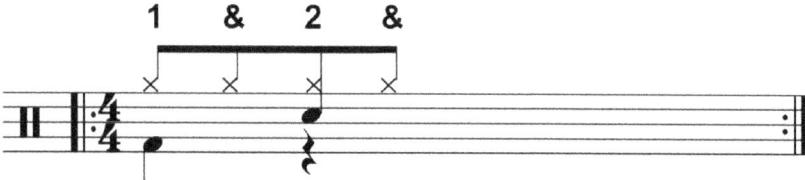

Continue this way until you've learned the entire groove.

As a side note, this is also a great technique for memorizing entire songs, learning the song measure by measure until you've memorized the whole song.

Sometimes the technique that works best for you depends on the beat you're trying to learn. If you're struggling with a groove, try learning it a different way. Eventually, it'll stick (pun intended).

Chart-Topping Drum Beats 1 – *The 60s Through Today*

OTHER CONSIDERATIONS

Focusing On The Feel

As you're learning a new beat, it's important to pay close attention to what the groove feels like as you play. The word *feel* in music often expresses certain emotions that the music triggers, but in this case I'm talking about the physical sense of the word. What does it actually feel like when you play it?

You can probably make the controller for your T.V. or game console do whatever you want without having to look at it. You know it by feel, which means you can get it to do what you want quickly and without much thought. In drumming, learning the feel of certain patterns makes it a much quicker process when learning new grooves that contain those patterns.

It's easy to get so caught up in staring at the music on the page that you almost completely ignore the way the groove feels. A great technique to help focus on the feel is to try to play the groove without looking at the music. When you do this, you're not only imagining the groove in your mind, but you're forced to focus your thoughts on your body movements. Once you know the feel of the groove, you own it, and the next time it comes around in your drumming endeavors, you'll be able to reproduce that feel very quickly.

The Art Of Listening

If you have the opportunity to listen to the groove you're trying to learn, this can help you grasp it more quickly. Try to imagine yourself playing the groove as you listen. Listen enough to get the groove "stuck" in your head to the point where you're able to sound out the groove in your mind without actually having to hear it.

Also, pay close attention to what the groove sounds like as *you* play it, which is easier said than done. You might find that once you start *really* listening to yourself play the groove, you fall apart, especially when learning a new groove. Fortunately, we have handy recording gadgets all over the place. Whip out your cell phone and record yourself playing. You'll often notice things that need to be improved that you couldn't hear while playing.

Simply listening to a groove is probably not enough to pick up a new beat, especially if it requires some coordinational skills that you haven't mastered yet. Used in combination with other learning techniques, listening is a powerful learning tool.

Building Muscle Memory

Great drummers all have one thing in common: they've played certain licks, combinations and patterns so many times that they've developed what's called *muscle memory* for those particular movements. Muscle memory is built through repetition and allows a drummer to perform movements without any conscious effort. Have you ever watched a great drummer playing and thought, "He/She makes it look so easy"? It looks easy because it actually is for him/her. There's no conscious effort because of the muscle memory built.

In this book, there are many coordination exercises, which are designed to gradually improve your coordination by building muscle memory. Each lesson in this book explores a new concept, which builds from the material in the previous lessons. As you work through the book, you'll find you're able to learn new beats faster and faster.

Lesson 2

8th Beat

INTRO TO 8th BEAT

LESSON 2 — 8th BEAT

If you want to be a successful drummer, the first step is to master the *8th beat* technique. It's the foundation for many of the drum beats you will encounter in popular music and is found in numerous songs from the 60s through today.

This technique gets its name because every stroke of the groove falls directly in-line with the 8th notes being played on the hi-hat. If you find yourself playing a bass or snare stroke that isn't in sync with the hi-hat, you're playing it incorrectly.

Ostinato [os-ti-**nah**-toh]
An ostinato is the part of the groove that repeats over and over. All 8th beat grooves share the 8th note ostinato played with the right stick or the left stick if you're playing left-handed (see below).

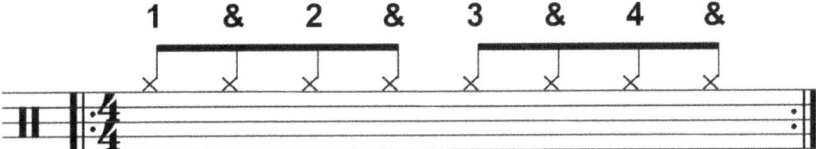

Popular 8th Beat Groove Examples
The "Mother Of All Rock Beats" from page 5 was your first 8th beat. To continue exploring 8th beat grooves, here are two popular songs also using this technique. These grooves are used in many songs from the 60s through today, but here are a few examples. Remember to consider the learning techniques explained in *Lesson 1* as you try to play these.

Sharp Dressed Man (verse & chorus)
ZZ Top (1983)
♩ = 125

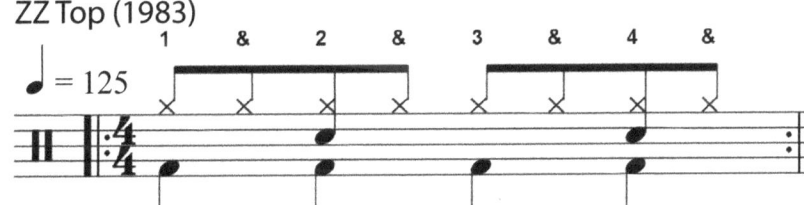

This groove is also used in *Take A Walk* – Passion Pit (2012) at 101 bpm.

Take It Easy (chorus)
The Eagles (1972)
♩ = 140

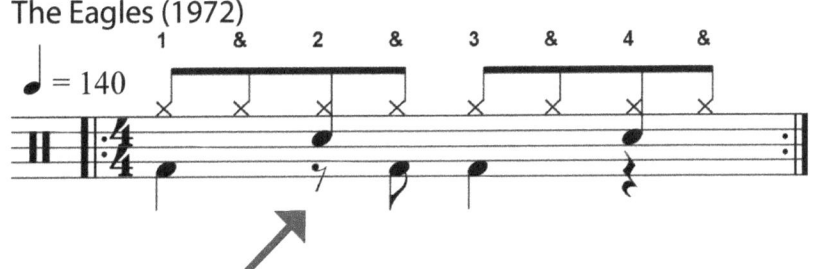

This groove is also used in *All I Want* – Toad The Wet Sprocket (1992) at 125 bpm.

8th rest. Do not strike the bass drum on a rest.

Chart-Topping Drum Beats 1 – The 60s Through Today

COORDINATION BUILDING

LESSON 2
8th BEAT

Now that you understand what the 8th beat technique is and how to read the notation, it's time to start building the muscle memory discussed in *Lesson 1*. These coordination exercises are designed to gradually build 8th beat coordination by building muscle memory through repetition.

Make sure you play along with a metronome to ensure you're playing the grooves in time. A fun practice technique is to play these exercises along with your favorite songs. Even though they may not be the exact beats played on the record, you'll be having a great time. Plus, the song takes the place of the metronome.

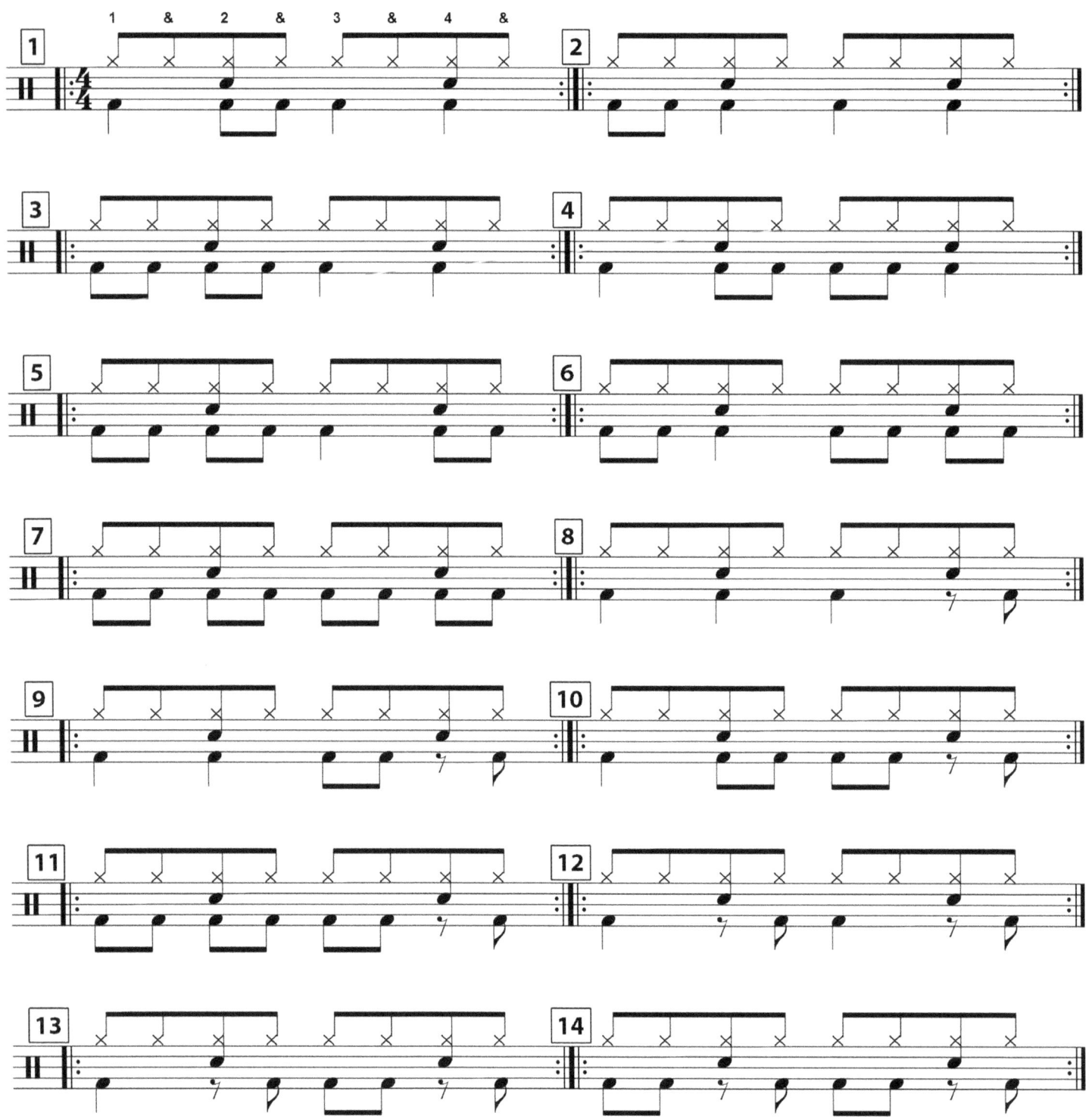

Chart-Topping Drum Beats 1 – *The 60s Through Today*

LESSON 2

COORDINATION BUILDING (cont.)

8th BEAT

The following grooves contain more 8th rests and quarter rests. As strange as it may sound, sometimes it's harder to "rest" than to strike the drum because your body naturally wants to strike with your other limbs.

Chart-Topping Drum Beats 1 – *The 60s Through Today*

COORDINATION BUILDING (cont.)

LESSON 2
8th BEAT

Often times, drum beats are grouped into two-measure repeating patterns. Playing a two-measure pattern can make the groove sound more interesting and less repetitive. Try these out.

LESSON 2

CHART-TOPPERS

8th BEAT

This book is designed with an emphasis on communicating the importance of learning what you're learning. When you know why you're learning what you're learning, it really is a motivation. I've included a number of chart-topping songs that use the 8th beat technique so that you can understand not only its value but how it is used.

Because you spent time building 8th beat coordination, you will find learning the following beats much easier. The more you develop coordination, the quicker you'll be able to learn new things.

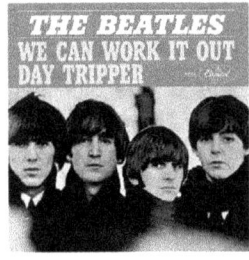

We Can Work It Out (verse)
The Beatles (1965)

♩ = 108

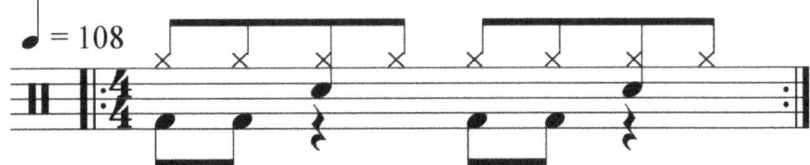

This groove is also used in *Yellow*– Coldplay (2000) at 87 bpm.

Jessie's Girl (chorus)
Rick Springfield (1981)

♩ = 132

This groove is also used in *I Melt With You*– Modern English (1982) at 156 bpm.

Shadow of the Day (chorus)
Linkin park (2007)

♩ = 110

Free Fallin' (verse)
Tom Petty (1989)

♩ = 85

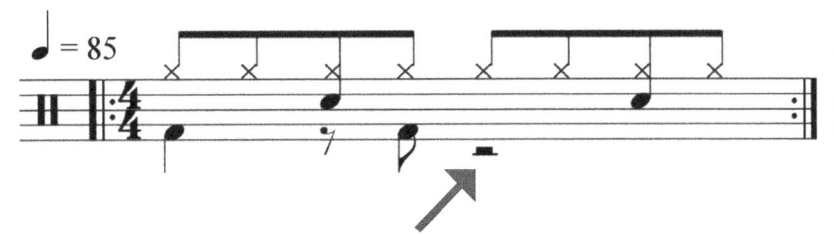

This groove is also used in *Pocket Full Of Sunshine*– Natasha Bedingfield (2007) at 139 bpm.

Half rest. Do not strike the bass drum on a rest.

Chart-Topping Drum Beats 1 – *The 60s Through Today*

CHART-TOPPERS (cont.)

LESSON 2
8th BEAT

You Really Got Me (intro & verse)
The Kinks (1964)

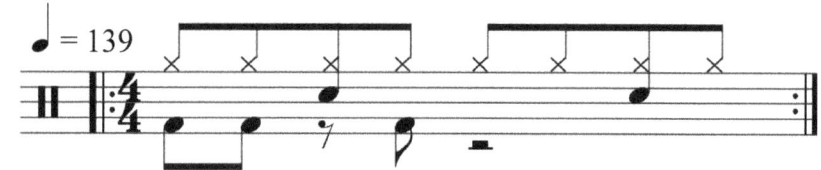

♩ = 139

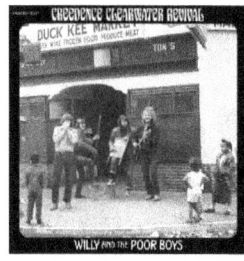

Feelin' Blue (intro, verse & chorus)
Creedence Clearwater Revival (1969)

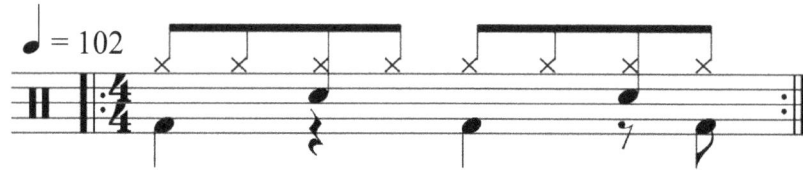

♩ = 102

This groove is also used in *Rock'n Me* – Steve Miller Band (1976) at 125 bpm.

Push (chorus 1st part)
Matchbox Twenty (1997)

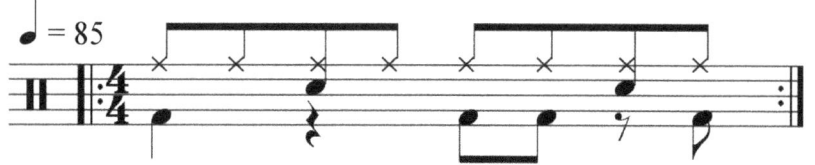

♩ = 85

This groove is also used in *For Your Love* – Yardbirds (1965) at 132 bpm.

We're An American Band (intro & chorus)
Grand Funk Railroad (1973)

♩ = 128

This groove is also used in *Sister Golden Hair* – America (1975) at 138 bpm.

Rock And Roll All Nite (verse)
Kiss (1975)

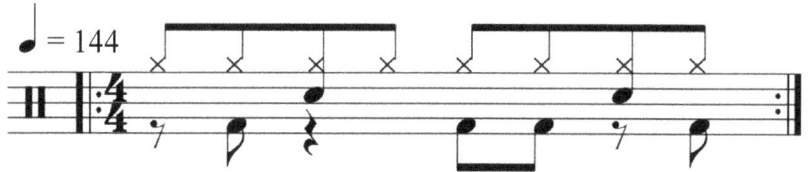

♩ = 144

Chart-Topping Drum Beats 1 – *The 60s Through Today*

CHART-TOPPERS (cont.)

LESSON 2 — 8th BEAT

Drummer:
Charlie Watts

Jumping Jack Flash (intro & chorus)
The Rolling Stones (1968)

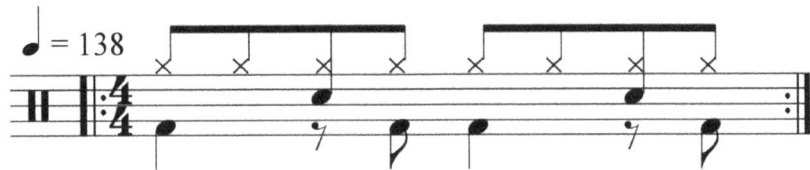

♩ = 138

This groove is also used in *Sweet Child O' Mine* – Guns N' Roses (1988) at 127 bpm.

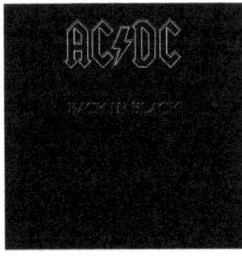

Drummer:
Phil Rudd

You Shook Me All Night Long (verse)
AC/DC (1980)

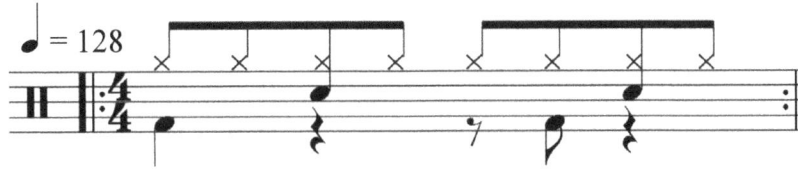

♩ = 128

This groove is also used in *Listen To Your Heart* – Roxette (1989) at 86 bpm.

Honky Tonk Women (verse)
The Rolling Stones (1969)

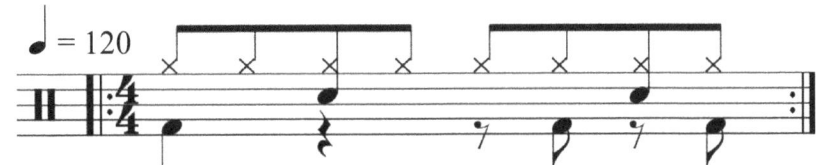

♩ = 120

Chart-Topping Drum Beats 1 – *The 60s Through Today*

CHART-TOPPERS (cont.)

LESSON 2
8th BEAT

The following chart-topping examples are two-measure repeating grooves. When working with 8th beat, two-measure repeating beats are common because they make the groove less repetitive. They are, however, more difficult to play because you have to remember more while playing.

After you've played the beat a few times through, try playing the groove without looking at the notation. This is a good listening exercise but also great practice for building your "beat memory." How many rock drummers do you see on stage reading sheet music? Probably not many!

Ohio (verse)
Crosby, Stills, Nash & Young (1970)

Livin' On A Prayer (intro)
Bon Jovi (1986)

The Middle (verse)
Jimmy Eat World (2001)

Long Cool Woman In A Black Dress (intro & re-intro)
The Hollies (1971)

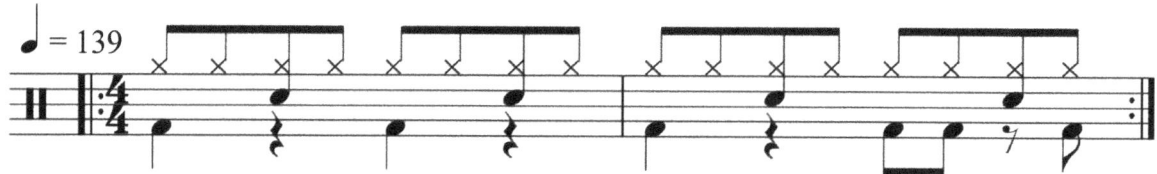

Chart-Topping Drum Beats 1 – *The 60s Through Today*

CHART-TOPPERS (cont.)

LESSON 2 — 8th BEAT

Since U Been Gone (verse)
Kelly Clarkson (2004)

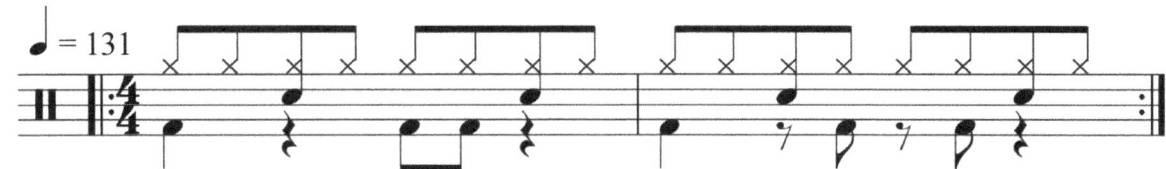
♩ = 131

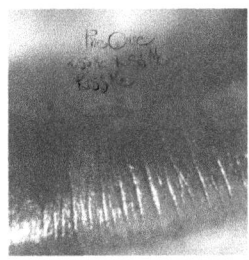

Just Like Heaven (intro & verse)
The Cure (1987)

♩ = 151

Come As You Are (intro & verse)
Nirvana (1992)

♩ = 121

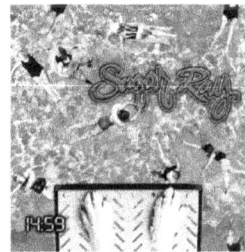

Every Morning (chorus)
Sugar Ray (1999)

♩ = 110

Please Don't Leave Me (verse & chorus)
Pink (2009)

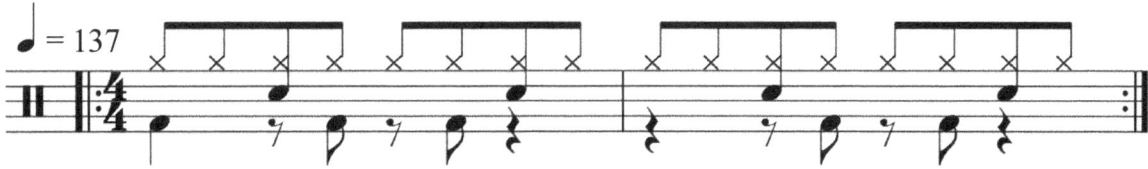
♩ = 137

Chart-Topping Drum Beats 1 – *The 60s Through Today*

CHART-TOPPERS (cont.)

LESSON 2

8th BEAT

What A Fool Believes (verse)
The Doobie Brothers (1979)

♩ = 123

We Built This City (verse)
Starship (1985)

♩ = 146

Original Prankster (intro & chorus)
The Offspring (2000)

♩ = 147

Kokomo (chorus)
The Beach Boys (1988)

♩ = 116

Get The Party Started (verse & chorus)
Pink (2001)

♩ = 129

Chart-Topping Drum Beats 1 – *The 60s Through Today*

CHART-TOPPERS (cont.)

LESSON 2 — 8th BEAT

Every Breath You Take (verse)
The Police (1975)

Hang On Sloopy (verse)
The McCoys (1965)

Run Around (2nd part of verse)
Blues Traveler (1994)

Life In Technicolor II (intro & verse)
Coldplay (2008)

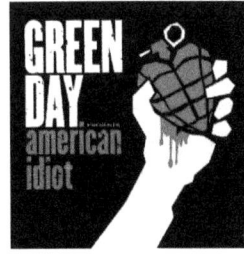

American Idiot (intro & verse)
Green Day (2004)

Chart-Topping Drum Beats 1 – *The 60s Through Today*

CHART-TOPPERS (cont.)

LESSON 2

8th BEAT

The first two chart-topping examples on this page include multiple measures of 8th note phrasing. The final example includes a crash cymbal. Be sure to keep solid timing when moving to the crash and back again to the hi-hat. Keep it consistent!

Hey Jealousy (verse)
Gin Blossoms (1993)

Born To Be Wild (verse)
Steppenwolf (1968)

If You Could Only See (intro)
Tonic (1997)

Chart-Topping Drum Beats 1 – *The 60s Through Today*

LESSON 2

COMPOSITION

8th BEAT

Writing a drum beat is fun. It's also something that many working drummers will find themselves having to do at some point in their career. Experiment with writing two-measure repeating beats below like you played throughout this lesson. Remember, not every rhythm you write will be your favorite, but the more you write, the better you'll become at finding great combinations to create the sound you're looking for.

DIRECTIONS: Write bass strokes to create your own 8th beats below.

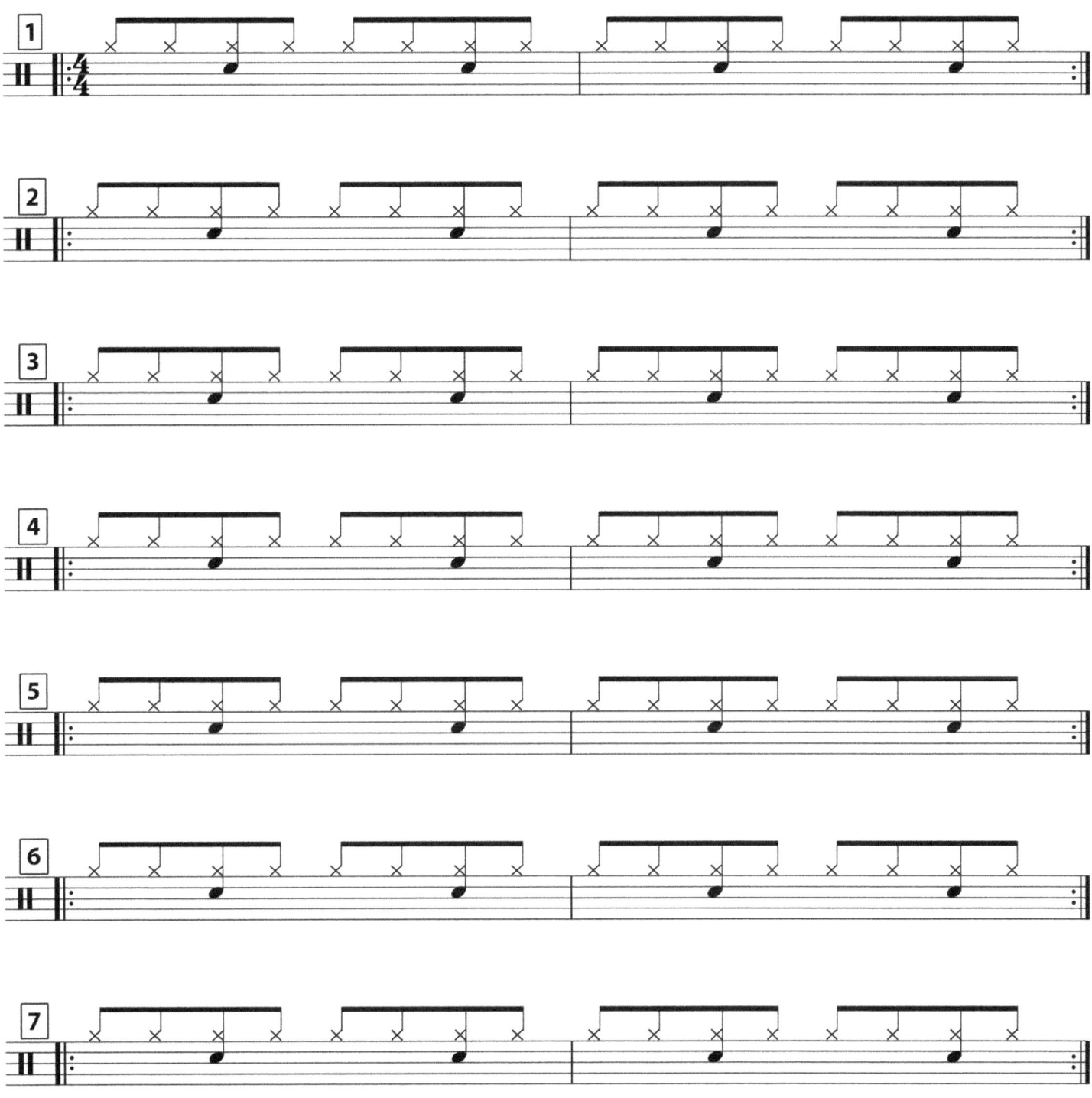

Chart-Topping Drum Beats 1 – *The 60s Through Today*

Lesson 3

Snare Movement

INTRO TO SNARE MOVEMENT

LESSON 3

While the snare drum is often played on beats "2" and "4", there are many songs that use additional snare drum strokes or that move the stroke away from "2" and/or "4" altogether. It's important to become comfortable with these techniques and the unique feel they create. This lesson explores techniques for moving the snare around 8th beat grooves.

Additional Snare Technique

Grooves are sometimes embellished by adding snare strokes, while keeping the snare strokes on beats "2" and "4." By doing this, the overall feel of the groove is changed but not dramatically.

Play the following rhythm, and then embellish it with an additional snare, as done in
Surfin' USA—The Beach Boys (1963).

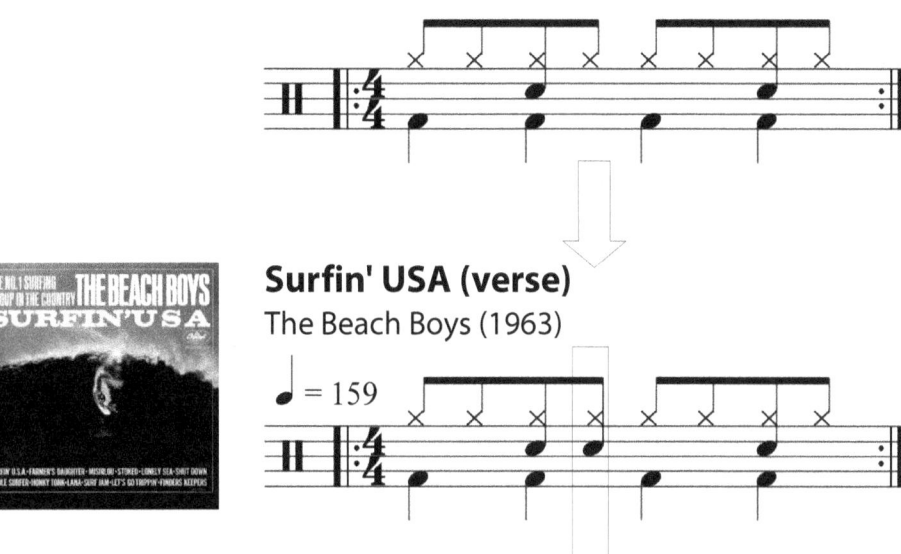

Surfin' USA (verse)
The Beach Boys (1963)

♩ = 159

Snare Displacement Technique

When the snare stroke is moved from the "2" and/or "4" it's called *displacement*. This technique often dramatically changes the feel of the groove. See how the feel of the groove changes when the snare is displaced like in *Beast Of Burden*—The Rolling Stones (1978).

Beast Of Burden (intro & 1st part of verse)
The Rolling Stones (1978)

♩ = 100

Chart-Topping Drum Beats 1 – *The 60s Through Today*

COORDINATION BUILDING

LESSON 3

SNARE MOVEMENT

The following exercises are designed to gradually build the coordination of adding an additional snare stroke.

This page focuses on adding a snare stroke on the "&" of beat "2". This particular hand pattern was very popular during the 60s surf music craze. *Pipeline*—The Chantays (1962), *Wipe Out*—The Surfaris (1963) and *Surf City*—Jan & Dean (1963) are just a few examples. Recently, The Black Keys surfed this hand pattern all the way to the top of the charts with their hit single, *Lonely Boy* (2012).

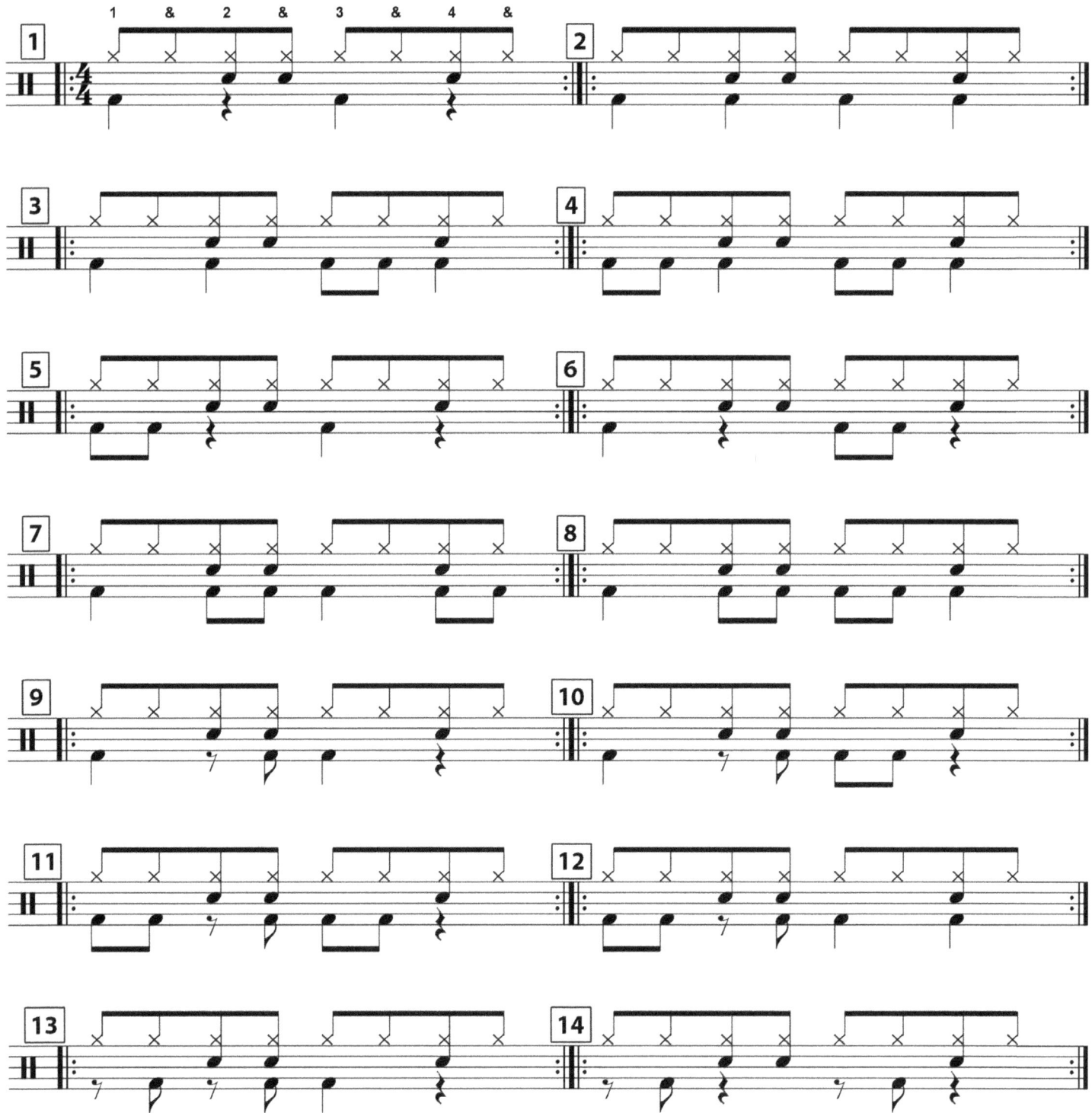

Chart-Topping Drum Beats 1 – *The 60s Through Today*

COORDINATION BUILDING (cont.)

LESSON 3

SNARE MOVEMENT

Flipping around the popular "surf" pattern from the previous exercises brings a slightly different feel to the groove. Try these exercises with the additional snare placed after the "4" instead of the "2."

Chart-Topping Drum Beats 1 – *The 60s Through Today*

COORDINATION BUILDING (cont.)

LESSON 3

SNARE MOVEMENT

You can change the feel of the groove yet again by placing the snare drum before the "4" instead of after. Try these exercises, and pay close attention to the feel this hand pattern creates.

COORDINATION BUILDING (cont.)

LESSON 3

SNARE MOVEMENT

A groove becomes **syncopated** when a normally "strong" beat becomes weak and vice versa. These exercises displace the snare to the "&" of "4." Pay close attention to the effect this pattern has on the feel.

COORDINATION BUILDING (cont.)

LESSON 3

SNARE MOVEMENT

Displacing the snare to before the "4" creates another syncopated pattern. Try these exercises and note the effect this pattern has on the grooves' feel.

Chart-Topping Drum Beats 1 – *The 60s Through Today*

LESSON 3

CHART-TOPPERS

SNARE MOVEMENT

The following chart-topping songs use snare movement techniques to bring a different feel to the music. Since you worked on developing coordination using this technique, you'll find a lot of these beats rather simple; however, you will also be introduced to new snare placements. Take these slowly at first while building your coordination.

Along with learning these beats, be sure to listen to each song so you can study the overall feel these beats bring to the piece. Also, note the variety of songs that use this technique.

The exercises on this page focus on the "surf" hand pattern you practiced on page 26.

For Your Love (verse & chorus)
The Yardbirds (1965)

♩ = 190

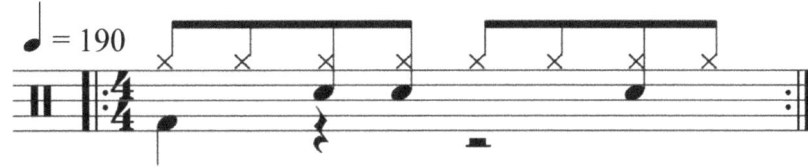

Stay (verse & chorus)
Maurice Williams And The Zodiacs (1960)

♩ = 121

The Loco-Motion (post-chorus)
Grand Funk Railroad (1974)

♩ = 127

This groove is also used in *Miserlou*– Dick Dale (1962) at 172 bpm.

Surfin' Bird (verse)
The Trashmen (1963)

♩ = 200

Chart-Topping Drum Beats 1 – *The 60s Through Today*

CHART-TOPPERS (cont.)

The chart-topping examples on this page use the snare displacement technique to change the backbeat.

Oxford Comma (intro & verse)
Vampire Weekend (2008)

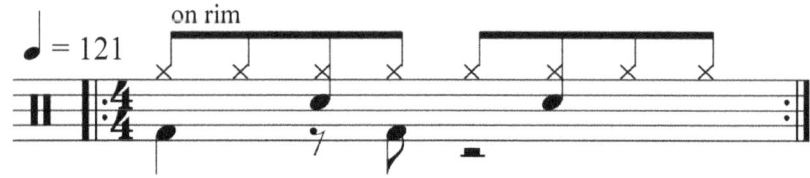

What I've Done (verse)
Linkin Park (2007)

Light My Fire (verse)
The Doors (1967)

Take My Breath Away (verse & chorus)
Berlin (1986)

This groove is also used in *Day After Day* – Badfinger (1971) at 102 bpm.

Clocks (verse)
Coldplay (2002)

Chart-Topping Drum Beats 1 – *The 60s Through Today*

CHART-TOPPERS (cont.)

The chart-topping examples on this page have the snare drum on all the downbeats (i.e. 1, 2, 3, 4). This creates an interesting feel that drives the song in a unique way.

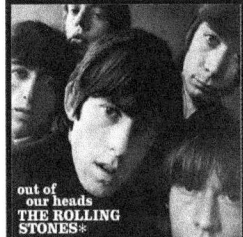

(I Can't Get No) Satisfaction (verse & chorus)
The Rolling Stones (1965)

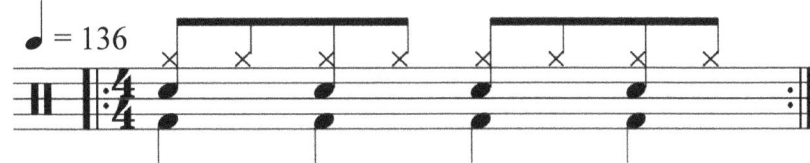

This groove is also used in *Band Of Gold*– Freda Payne (1970) at 109 bpm.

California Dreamin' (chorus)
The Mamas & The Papas (1965)

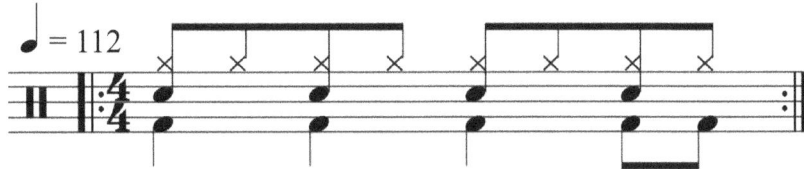

Born To Be Wild (post-chorus & middle)
Steppenwolf (1968)

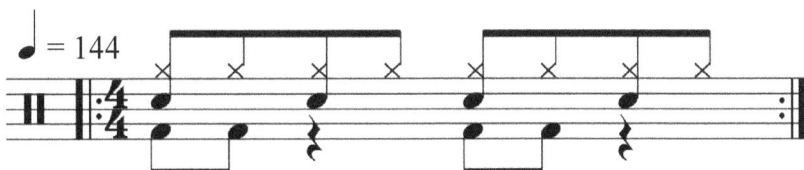

Purple Haze (intro)
The Jimi Hendrix Experience (1967)

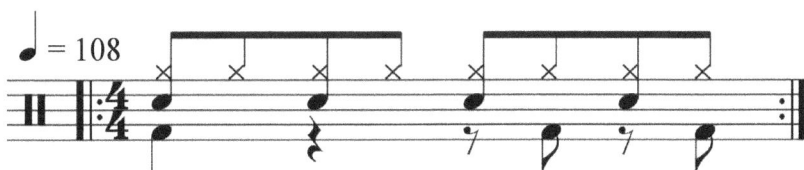

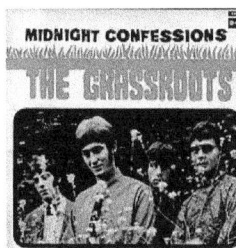

Midnight Confessions (verse & chorus)
The Grass Roots (1968)

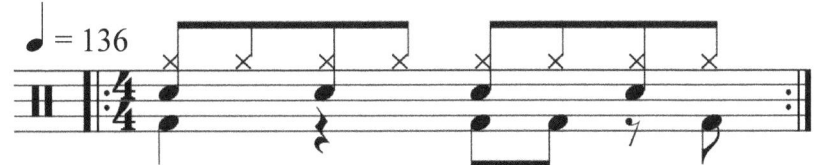

This groove is also used in *I Can't Help Myself (Sugar Pie Honey Bunch)*– The Four Tops (1965) at 128 bpm.

Chart-Topping Drum Beats 1 – *The 60s Through Today*

CHART-TOPPERS (cont.)

LESSON 3

SNARE MOVEMENT

These chart-topping examples use two-measure repeating patterns to make the grooves more interesting.

Zombie (intro & chorus)
The Cranberries (1994)

Song 2 (verse)
Blur (1997)

Feel Again (final chorus)
OneRepublic (2012)

Twist And Shout (chorus)
The Beatles (1964)

Good (intro)
Better Than Ezra (1993)

Chart-Topping Drum Beats 1 – *The 60s Through Today*

CHART-TOPPERS (cont.)

The last two examples on this page are four-measure repeating patterns. Take them slowly at first and build your speed. Then, try turning away from the notation and play from memory.

All My Life (verse)
Foo Fighters (2002)

Be My Baby (verse)
The Ronettes (1963)

It's My Party (chorus)
Lesley Gore (1963)

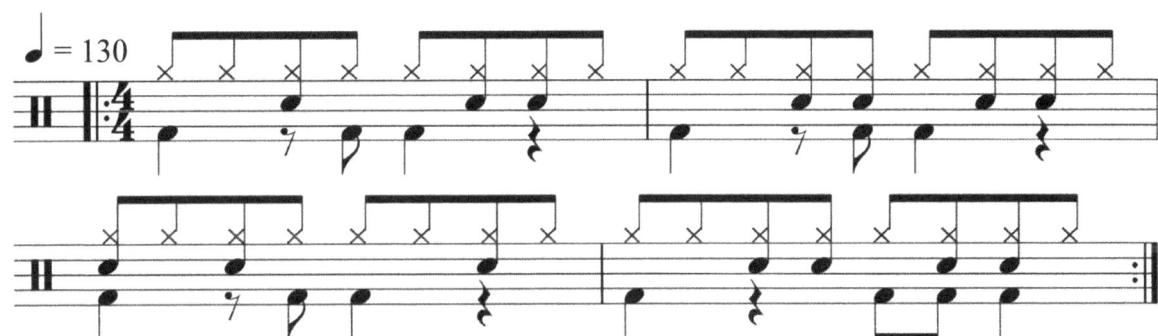

All Along The Watchtower (intro)
The Jimi Hendrix Experience (1968)

Chart-Topping Drum Beats 1 – *The 60s Through Today*

COMPOSITION

LESSON 3

SNARE MOVEMENT

Continue working on your writing skills. Get creative! The more you explore snare placements, the better you'll become at creating the sounds you like.

Be sure to play each beat as you write it. This is a good assignment to do with a pencil (and an extra eraser or two) while sitting behind the kit to test them out.

DIRECTIONS: Write snare strokes below using the *additional snare* & *displacement* techniques.

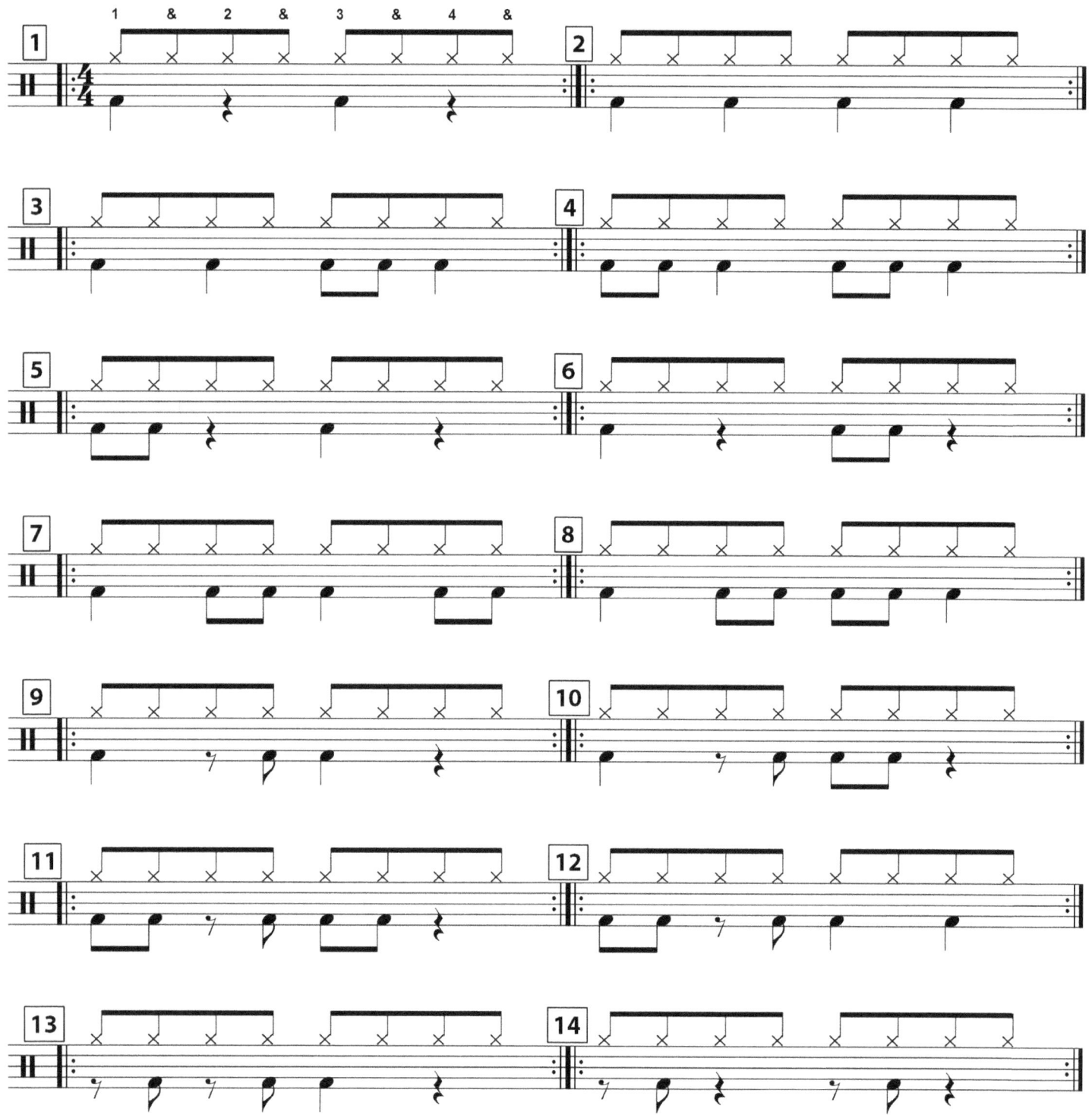

Chart-Topping Drum Beats 1 – *The 60s Through Today*

Lesson 4

16th Note Bass Phrasing

INTRO TO 16th NOTE BASS PHRASING

LESSON 4

So far, all of the rhythms you've practiced have snare and bass strokes that fall directly in line with the hi-hat strokes. Many drum beats use **sixteenth-note phrasing**, which is the technique of placing strokes in-between the 8th notes on the hi-hat strokes (i.e. on the "e" and/or "ah"). It's important to keep your 8th notes on the hi-hat very consistent. Developing good timing is essential to your success as a drummer.

Bass Drum: The Heart Beat

The bass drum is the heart beat of a song. The audience can feel it thump in their chest as they listen. Your bass drum needs to drive the song in a meaningful way. This section of the book introduces a lot of different patterns for the bass, but it's important to remember that bass-rich patterns shouldn't be used just for the sake of having more bass. As a drummer, it's your job to *find* the beat that brings the song to life.

As a side note, as you listen to songs, you'll notice that a lot of times there is a specific "heart beat" for each section of the song (i.e. verse, intro, chorus, etc.). Try listening to how the bass patterns change in your favorite songs as they progress through different sections.

Sixteenth-Note Phrasing With The Bass Drum

Sixteenth-note phrasing can be accomplished by placing a bass stroke in between the hi-hats. Check out how this technique is used in *Jane Says*—Jane's Addiction (1988).

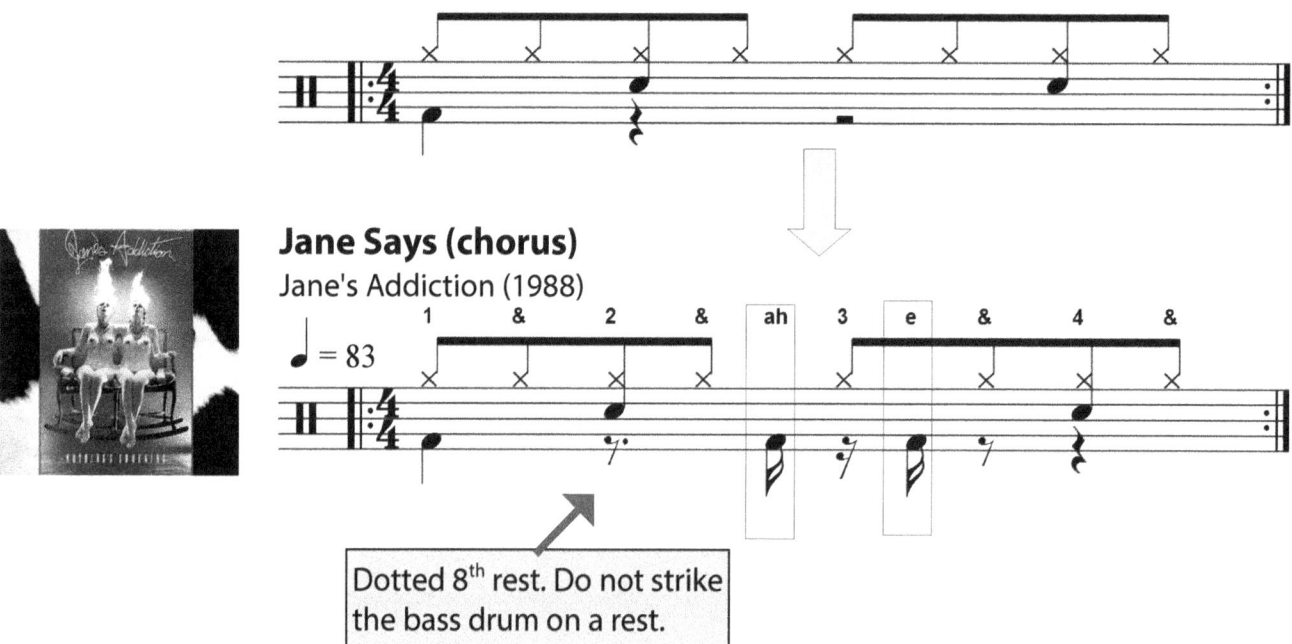

Jane Says (chorus)
Jane's Addiction (1988)

Dotted 8th rest. Do not strike the bass drum on a rest.

Chart-Topping Drum Beats 1 – *The 60s Through Today*

COORDINATION BUILDING

LESSON 4
16th BASS PHRASING

The first set of exercises focuses on adding an "ah" on the bass drum in-between the hi-hat strokes. Take your time with these because you'll run into these types of grooves all throughout your drumming career.

Chart-Topping Drum Beats 1 – *The 60s Through Today*

COORDINATION BUILDING (cont.)

LESSON 4 — 16th BASS PHRASING

These exercises are designed to develop coordination for playing the bass drum on the "e." While playing, make sure your hi-hat strokes stay consistent. Also, listen to the difference in feel this pattern creates.

COORDINATION BUILDING (cont.)

LESSON 4 — 16th BASS PHRASING

These exercises incorporate bass strokes on both the "e" and "ah." Some of these can be tiring on your bass drum foot. Start slowly, and gradually build speed with time. Eventually, you'll have built endurance.

Chart-Topping Drum Beats 1 – *The 60s Through Today*

CHART-TOPPERS

LESSON 4

16" BASS PHRASING

Sixteenth-note phrasing opens up a lot of possibilities because it creates twice as many stroke options for each limb. These chart-topping examples show how this technique has been used throughout the years and also exemplify the wide range of styles that use sixteenth-note phrasing.

In addition to playing these grooves, listen to the songs. Pay close attention to the overall feel of the song. Being able to play the beats is one thing, but understanding how they are used and what they bring to a song in terms of feel is very important.

We Are Family (verse & chorus)
Sister Sledge (1979)

This groove is also used in *Shining Star*– Earth, Wind & Fire (1975) at 103 bpm.

Paradise City (verse)
Guns N' Roses (1988)

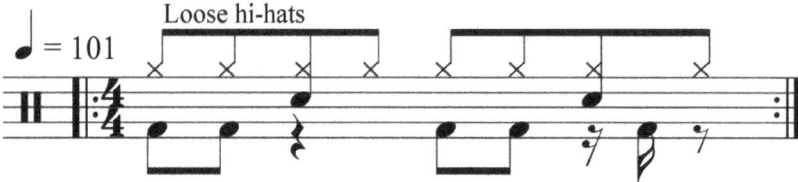

I Alone (chorus)
Live (1994)

Creep (verse & chorus)
Stone Temple Pilots (1993)

Chart-Topping Drum Beats 1 – *The 60s Through Today*

CHART-TOPPERS (cont.)

LESSON 4 — 16th BASS PHRASING

Heartbreaker (intro & re-intro)
Led Zeppelin (1970)

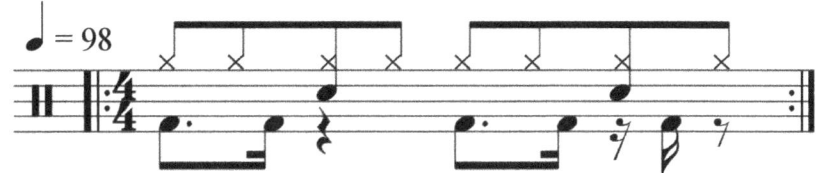

Losing A Whole Year (verse)
Third Eye Blind (1998)

This groove is also used in *Creep*– Radiohead (1992) at 93 bpm.

Soul Man (verse)
Sam And Dave (1967)

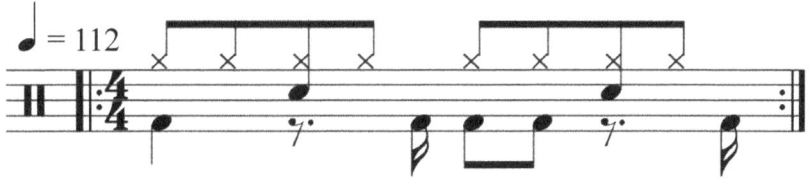

Simple Man (verse)
Lynyrd Skynyrd (1973)

Hemorrhage (In My Hands) (chorus & middle)
Fuel (2000)

This groove is also used in *Far Behind*– Candlebox (1994) at 90 bpm.

Chart-Topping Drum Beats 1 – *The 60s Through Today*

CHART-TOPPERS (cont.)

LESSON 4
16th BASS PHRASING

Whatever It Takes (verse)
Lifehouse (2007)

This groove is also used in *Drive* – Incubus (2000) at 90 bpm.

Pour Some Sugar On Me (intro & verse)
Def Leppard (1987)

I Want You Back (chorus)
The Jackson 5 (1969)

Ruby (verse & chorus)
Kaiser Chiefs (2007)

Can't You See (verse)
The Marshall Tucker Band (1973)

Chart-Topping Drum Beats 1 – *The 60s Through Today*

CHART-TOPPERS (cont.)

LESSON 4 — 16th BASS PHRASING

Lean On Me (verse & chorus)
Bill Withers (1972)

Mississippi Queen (verse)
Mountain (1970)

Over The Hills And Far Away (verse)
Led Zeppelin (1973)

Bully (verse)
Shinedown (2012)

Time (verse)
Pink Floyd (1974)

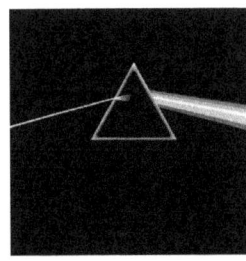
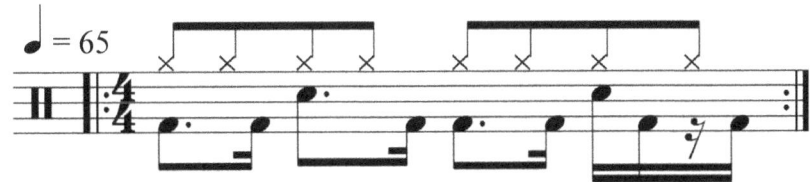

Chart-Topping Drum Beats 1 – *The 60s Through Today*

CHART-TOPPERS (cont.)

LESSON 4
16th BASS PHRASING

The examples on this page are two-measure repeating beats from chart-topping songs.

November Rain (guitar solo)
Guns N' Roses (1992)

Why Don't You Get A Job (intro)
The Offspring (1998)

Fat Bottomed Girls (1st chorus)
Queen (1978)

R U Mine? (2nd verse)
Arctic Monkeys (2012)

Epic (intro)
Faith No More (1990)

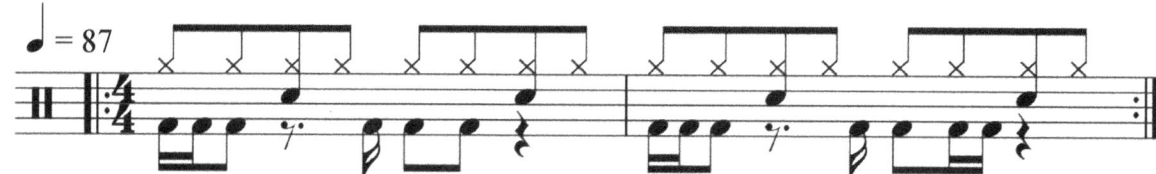

Chart-Topping Drum Beats 1 – *The 60s Through Today*

CHART-TOPPERS (cont.)

LESSON 4 — 16th BASS PHRASING

The examples on this page incorporate the snare movement techniques from *lesson 3* as well as sixteenth-note phrasing on the bass.

More Than A Feeling (chorus)
Boston (1976)

Bitter Sweet Symphony (verse & chorus)
The Verve (1997)

Ramble On (chorus)
Led Zeppelin (1969)

3AM (verse)
Matchbox Twenty (1997)

Chart-Topping Drum Beats 1 – *The 60s Through Today*

COMPOSITION

LESSON 4

16" BASS PHRASING

Continue working on your writing and creating skills with the template below. Tap out the rhythms or try them out on the kit as you write them. Make good use of your pencil's eraser if you come across something that doesn't work. Use this process to challenge yourself and to work on developing your own unique drumming style.

DIRECTIONS: Write bass strokes to create your own drum beats with sixteenth-note phrasing below.

Chart-Topping Drum Beats 1 – *The 60s Through Today*

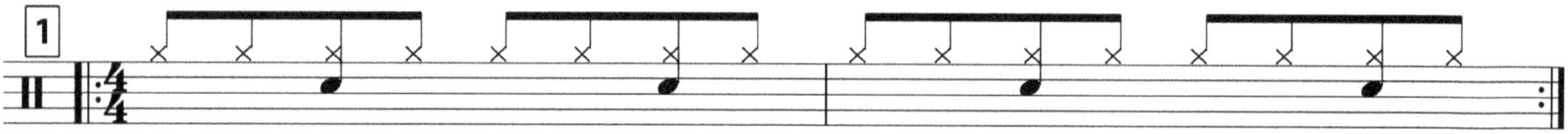

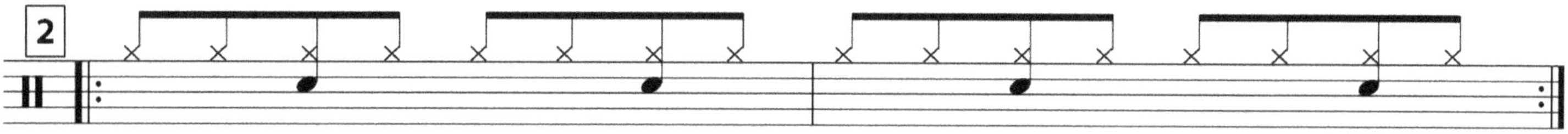

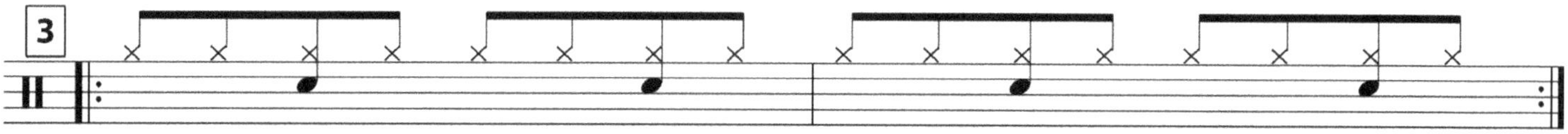

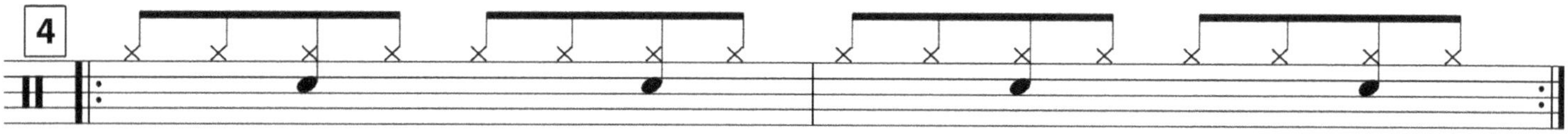

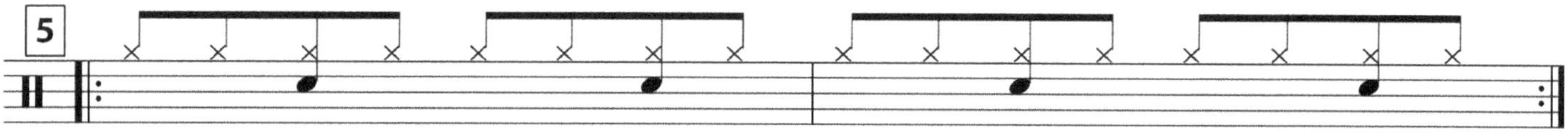

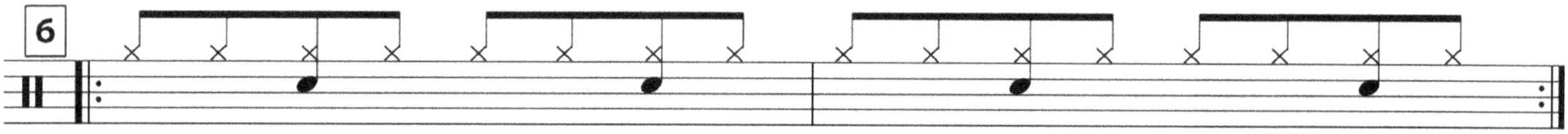

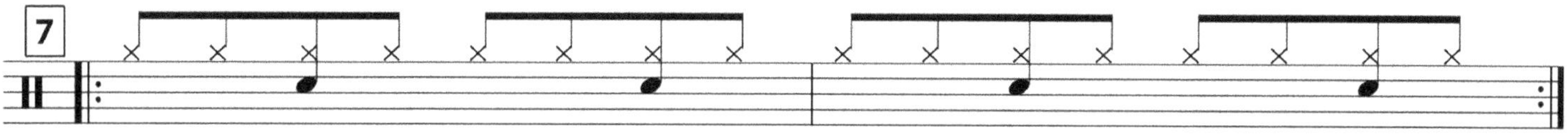

Lesson 5

16th Note Snare Phrasing

INTRO TO 16th SNARE PHRASING

So far, you've worked on sixteenth-note phrasing with the bass drum. This lesson explores sixteenth-note phrasing with the snare drum, as well as grooves that include both snare and bass drum phrasing.

Sixteenth-Note Phrasing With The Snare Drum

Sixteenth-note phrasing on the snare drum is often used as an embellishment technique while leaving the backbeat on "2" and "4." Doing this allows you to maintain the general feel of the 8th beat with a little extra flair. See how this technique is used in *Jumper*—Third Eye Blind (1997).

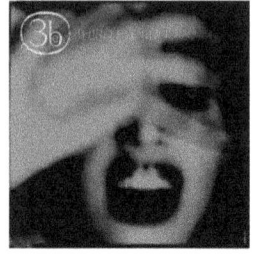
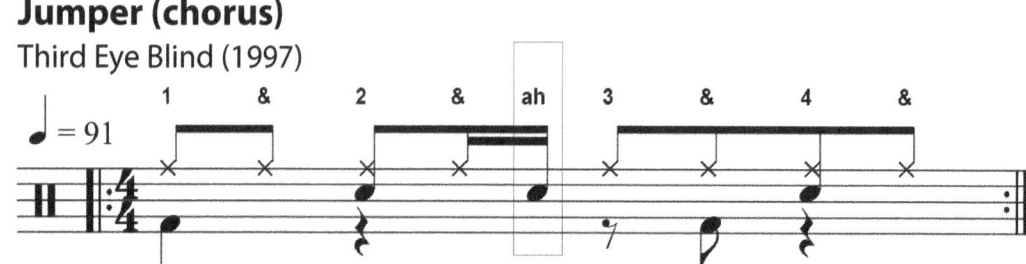

Jumper (chorus)
Third Eye Blind (1997)

Snare Displacement With Sixteenth-Note Phrasing

In lesson 3 you practiced displacing the snare with 8th beat grooves. You can also displace the snare to a sixteenth (i.e. on the "e" and/or "ah"). See how this technique is used in *Soul To Squeeze*—Red Hot Chili Peppers (1993).

Soul To Squeeze (verse)
Red Hot Chili Peppers (1993)

Sixteenth-Note Phrasing With Both The Snare Drum And Bass

The bass drum is often phrased in sixteenths to create a wide range of patterns. See how this technique is used in *I'm Bad, I'm Nationwide*—ZZ Top (1979).

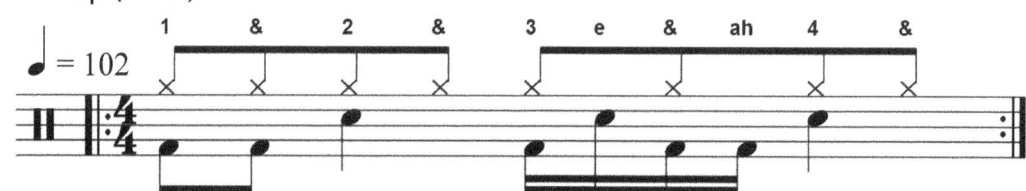

I'm Bad, I'm Nationwide (intro)
ZZ Top (1979)

Chart-Topping Drum Beats 1 – *The 60s Through Today*

COORDINATION BUILDING

LESSON 5

16th SNARE PHRASING

The first set of sixteenth-note phrasing exercises focuses on adding an "ah" after the "&" of "2." For now, we're using only 8th note phrasing on the bass drum so you can focus on the hands.

Chart-Topping Drum Beats 1 – *The 60s Through Today*

LESSON 5

COORDINATION BUILDING (cont.)

SNARE PHRASING

These exercises add an "ah" after the "&" of count "4" in addition the pattern you practiced on the previous page. This can create a repetitive sounding groove, which isn't always good, but it's not always bad, either.

Chart-Topping Drum Beats 1 – *The 60s Through Today*

COORDINATION BUILDING (cont.)

LESSON 5 — 16TH SNARE PHRASING

The grooves you've worked on so far have the snare phrased on the "ah." Now let's try some with the snare on the "e." As you play these, pay attention to the difference in feel the "e" brings to the beat.

Chart-Topping Drum Beats 1 – *The 60s Through Today*

COORDINATION BUILDING (cont.)

LESSON 5

16" SNARE PHRASING

The hand pattern on this page is based off of Clyde Stubblefield's famous groove from *Funky Drummer—James Brown* (1986). This groove became so widely sampled and played in the early 90s that it became somewhat of a musical cliché. Even though it's been played to death, it's an important groove in drumming history, and every drummer should learn to play it.

Chart-Topping Drum Beats 1 – *The 60s Through Today*

COORDINATION BUILDING (cont.)

LESSON 5
16th SNARE PHRASING

These exercises use sixteenth-note phrasing on both the snare and bass drum. With all the phrasing going on, it's easy to lose track of the 8th notes on the hi-hat. Focus on keeping the 8th notes consistent.

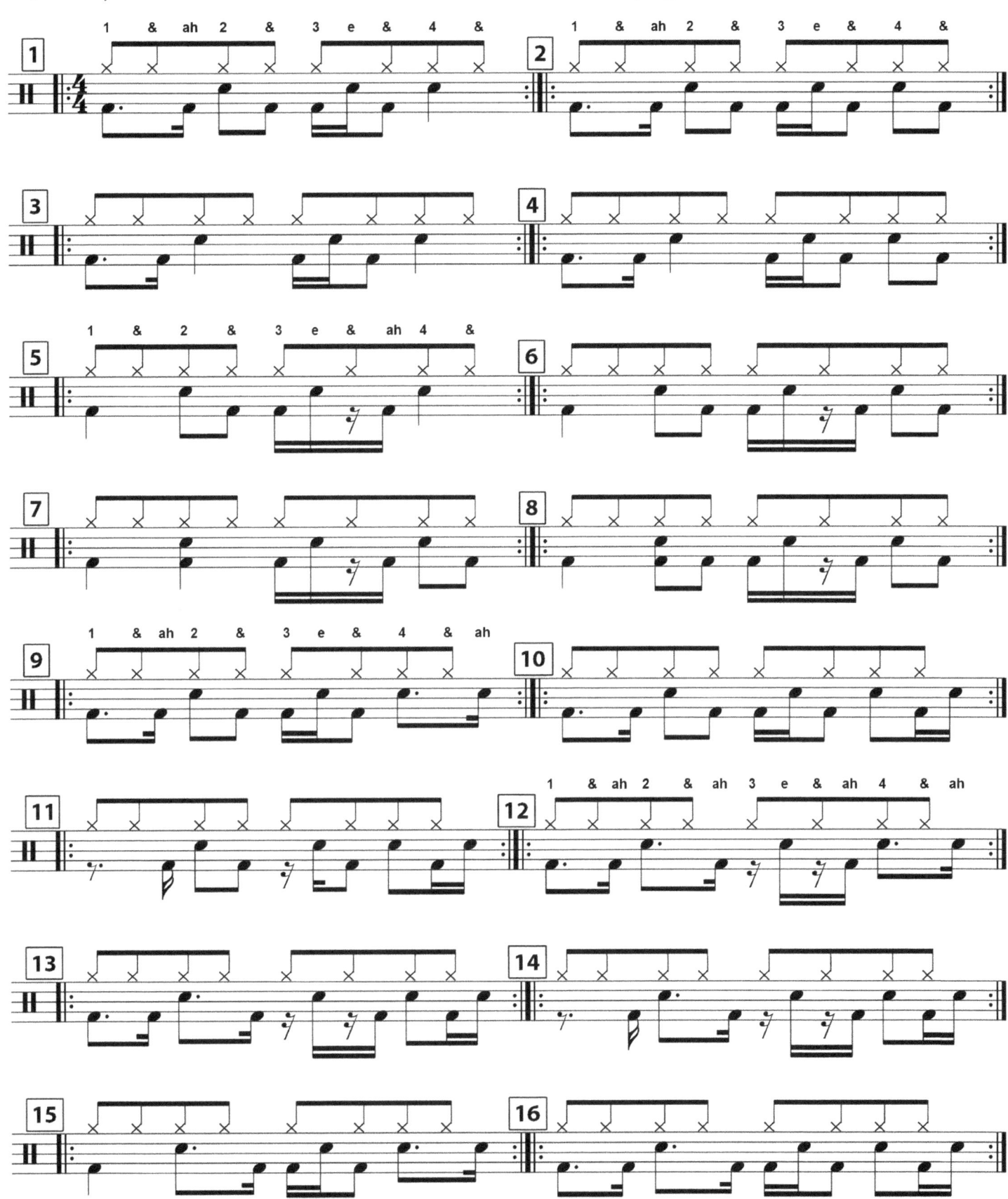

Chart-Topping Drum Beats 1 – *The 60s Through Today*

COORDINATION BUILDING (cont.)

LESSON 5

16th SNARE PHRASING

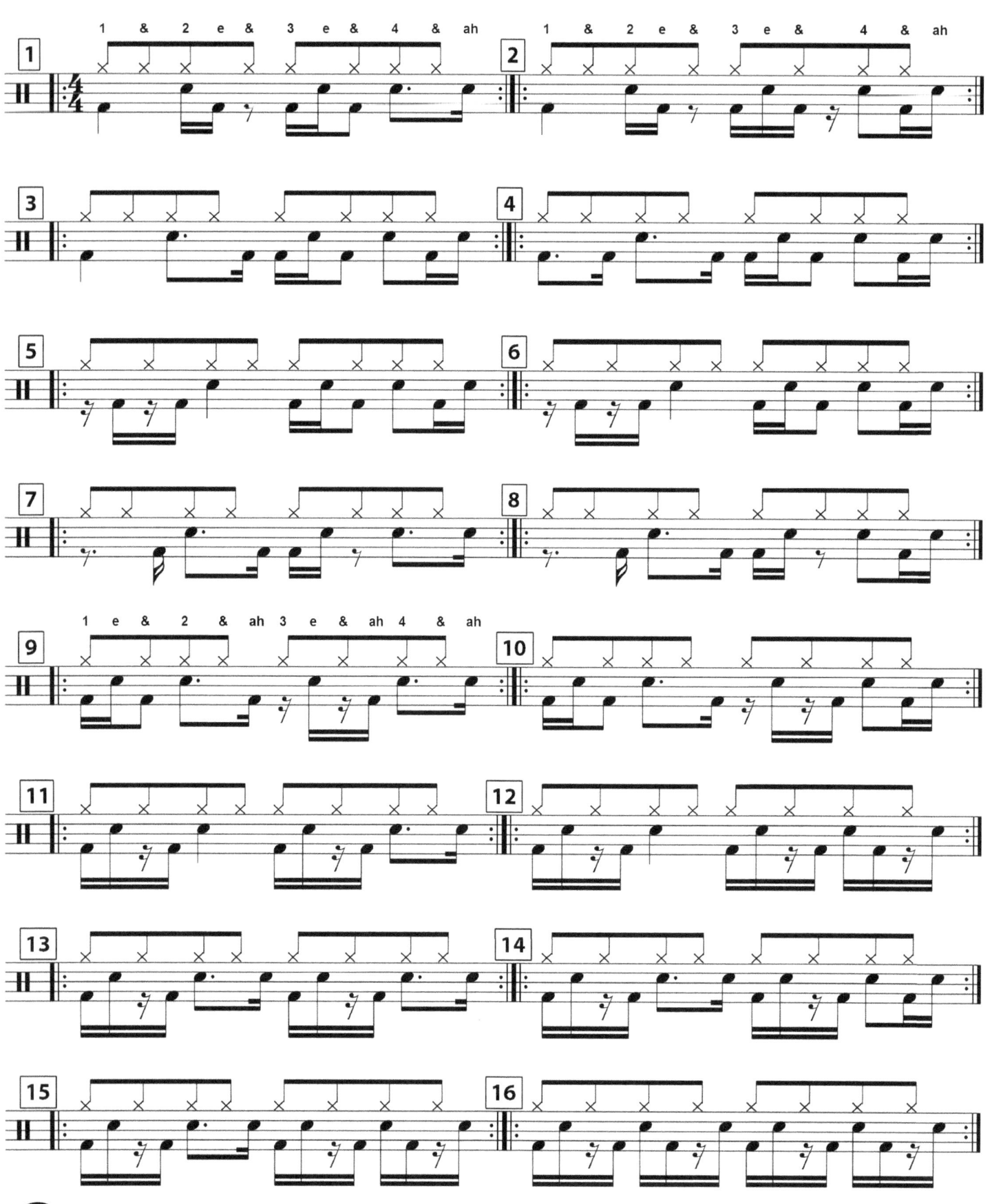

COORDINATION BUILDING (cont.)

LESSON 5

16th SNARE PHRASING

These exercises include bass patterns with two sixteenth notes in a row. Working up the speed and endurance to play quick strokes on the bass takes time. Start slowly and work your way up.

Chart-Topping Drum Beats 1 – *The 60s Through Today*

LESSON 5

CHART-TOPPERS

16TH SNARE PHRASING

The following examples include sixteenth-note phrasing on snare drum and/or bass drum.

I'm Every Woman (verse)
Chaka Khan (1978)

Panic Switch (verse)
Silversun Pickups (2009)

Machinehead (verse)
Bush (1996)

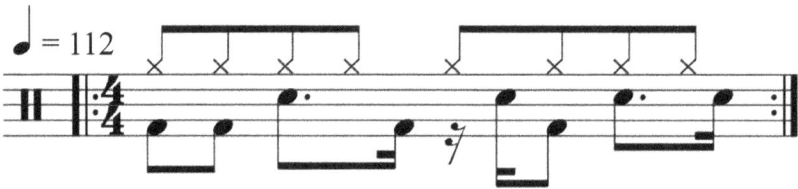

Absolutely (Story Of A Girl) (verse & chorus)
Nine Days (2000)

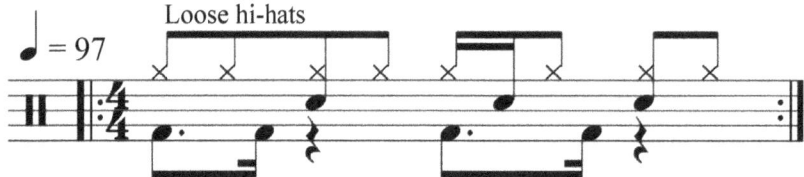

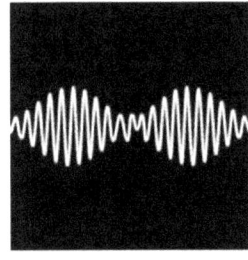

R U Mine? (chorus)
Arctic Monkeys (2012)

Chart-Topping Drum Beats 1 – *The 60s Through Today*

CHART-TOPPERS (cont.)

LESSON 5

By The Way (intro & pre-chorus)
Red Hot Chili Peppers (2002)

Someone To Save You (intro & chorus)
OneRepublic (2007)

Father Of Mine (chorus)
Everclear (1997)

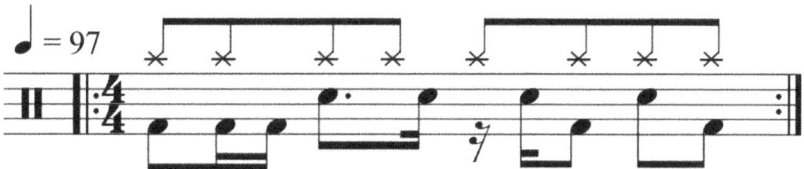

Tripin' On A Hole In A Paper Heart (verse)
Stone Temple Pilots (1996)

Shimmer (verse)
Fuel (1998)

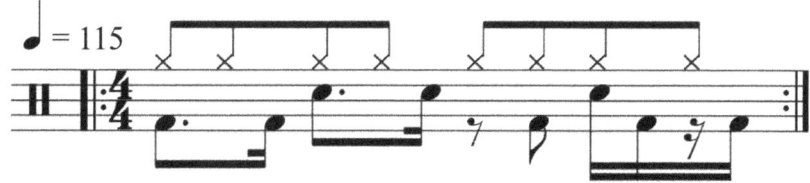

Chart-Topping Drum Beats 1 – *The 60s Through Today*

CHART-TOPPERS (cont.)

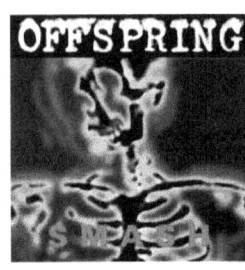

Self Esteem (verse)
Offspring (1994)

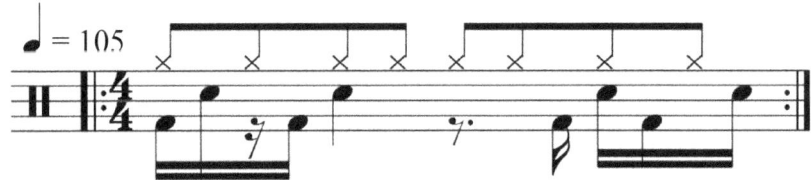

Be Like That (final chorus)
3 Doors Down (2000)

Sugar, We're Going Down (intro & chorus)
Fallout Boy (2005)

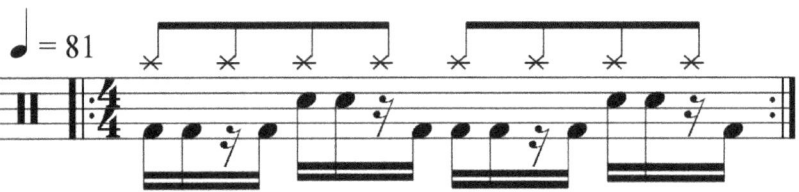

Clumsy (bridge to chorus)
Our Lady Peace (1997)

I Alone (chorus fill)
Live (1994)

Chart-Topping Drum Beats 1 – *The 60s Through Today*

CHART-TOPPERS (cont.)

LESSON 5
16th SNARE PHRASING

Why I'm Here (verse)
Oleander (1999)

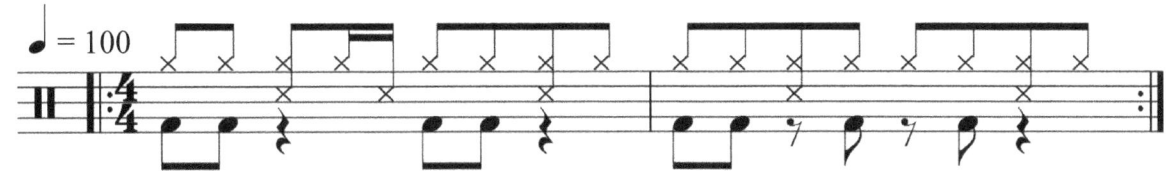

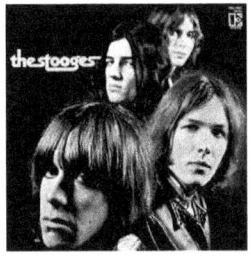

I Wanna Be Your Dog (verse)
The Stooges (1969)

Carry On My Wayward Son (post-chorus)
Kansas (1976)

Sooner Or Later (intro)
Breaking Benjamin (2004)

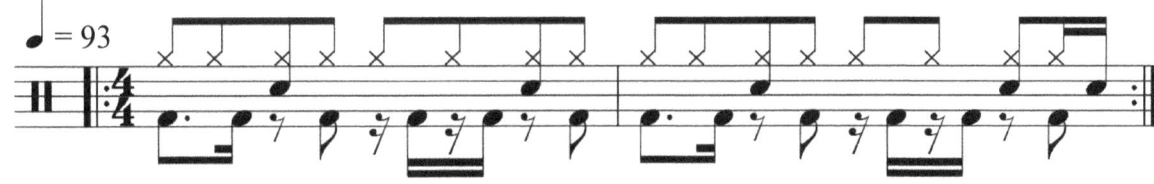

When I Come Around (verse)
Green Day (1995)

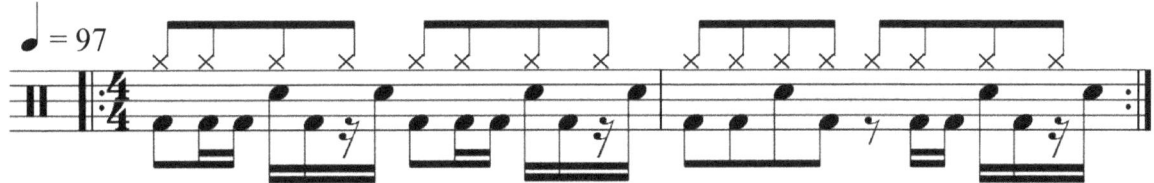

Chart-Topping Drum Beats 1 – *The 60s Through Today*

LESSON 5

COMPOSITION

SNARE PHRASING

Building the coordination to play other drummers' beats is good, but it's also important to write and play your own. Developing your own unique style can really make you stand out as a drummer. Below, experiment with writing drum beats using the sixteenth-note phrasing technique. Take your time, and make them sound cool!

PART A
DIRECTIONS: Write both snare and bass strokes using the sixteenth-note phrasing technique.

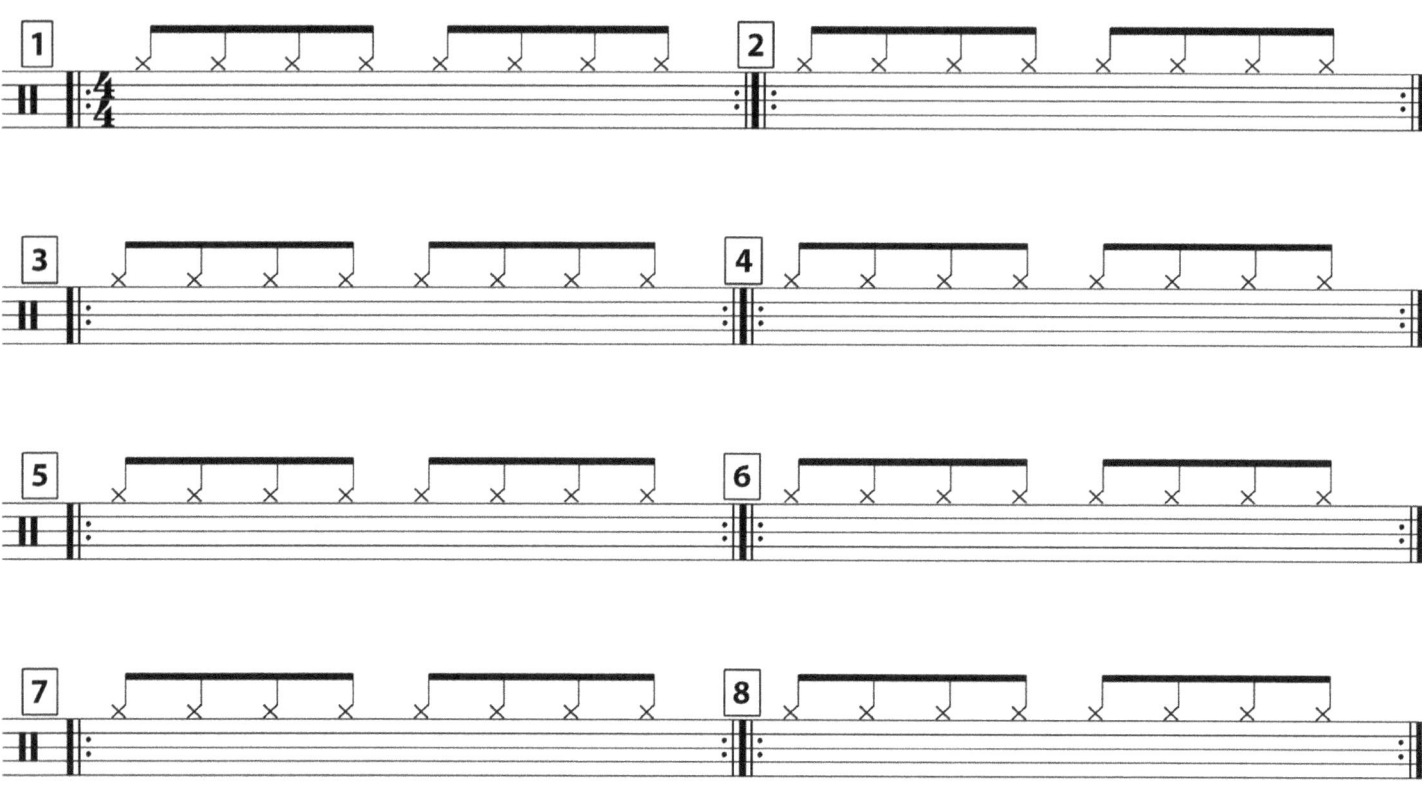

PART B
DIRECTIONS: Write both snare and bass strokes to make two-measure repeating beats using the sixteenth-note phrasing technique.

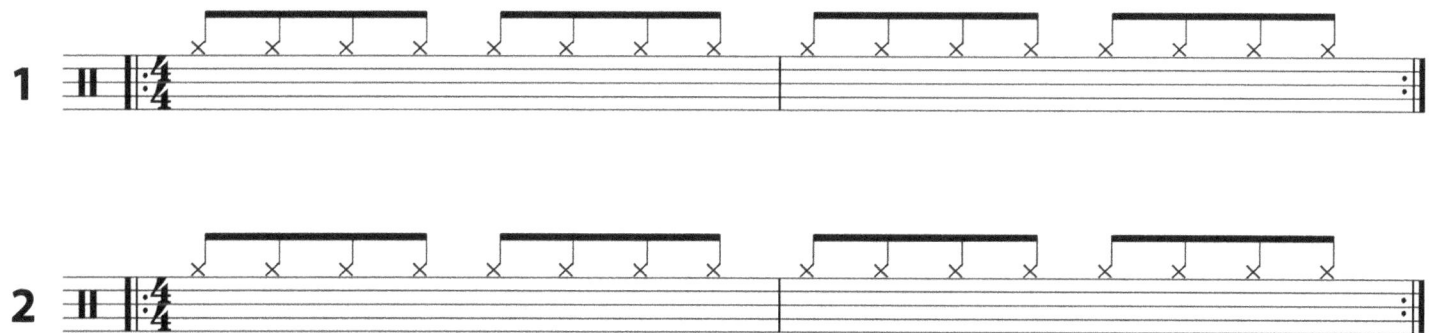

Chart-Topping Drum Beats 1 – *The 60s Through Today*

Lesson 6

Embellishing

LESSON 6
INTRO TO EMBELLISHING

EMBELLISHING

The word *embellish* means to make something more attractive by adding features and elements. There are a lot of things we can do as drummers, such as adding strokes, changing the volume, using different stroke types, opening the hi-hat, etc. In this lesson, we're going to focus on two embellishments: opening the hi-hat and ghost strokes.

Open Hi-Hat Technique

So far, we've used a closed hi-hat. It's time to open it! When a "**o**" is placed above a hi-hat stroke, it means to open it for that stroke. A "**+**" above the note indicates that the hi-hat should be closed again. Check out how it's used in the famous MTV song *Money For Nothing*—Dire Straits (1985).

Money For Nothing (2nd verse)
Dire Straits (1985)

Ghost-Stroke Technique

Another common embellishment technique is adding a **ghost stroke**, a very lightly hit stroke. Parentheses around a note indicate that the note should be played *ghosted*. The term **dynamics** refers to how loudly or softly you play. By changing the dynamics, such as using ghost strokes, you can really bring your grooves to life.

Check out how the ghosting technique is used in *Fly*—Sugar Ray (1997).

Fly (verse)
Sugar Ray (1997)

This groove is also used in *All Star*– Smash Mouth (1999) at 104 bpm.

Chart-Topping Drum Beats 1 – *The 60s Through Today*

COORDINATION BUILDING

LESSON 6 — EMBELLISHING

This section focuses on using the open hi-hat technique to embellish grooves. These are arranged with 8th beat grooves at first so that you can focus on becoming comfortable with the hi-hat foot.

Chart-Topping Drum Beats 1 – *The 60s Through Today*

COORDINATION BUILDING (cont.)

LESSON 6 — EMBELLISHING

These exercises incorporate sixteenth-note phrasing on the bass drum along with the open hi-hat technique.

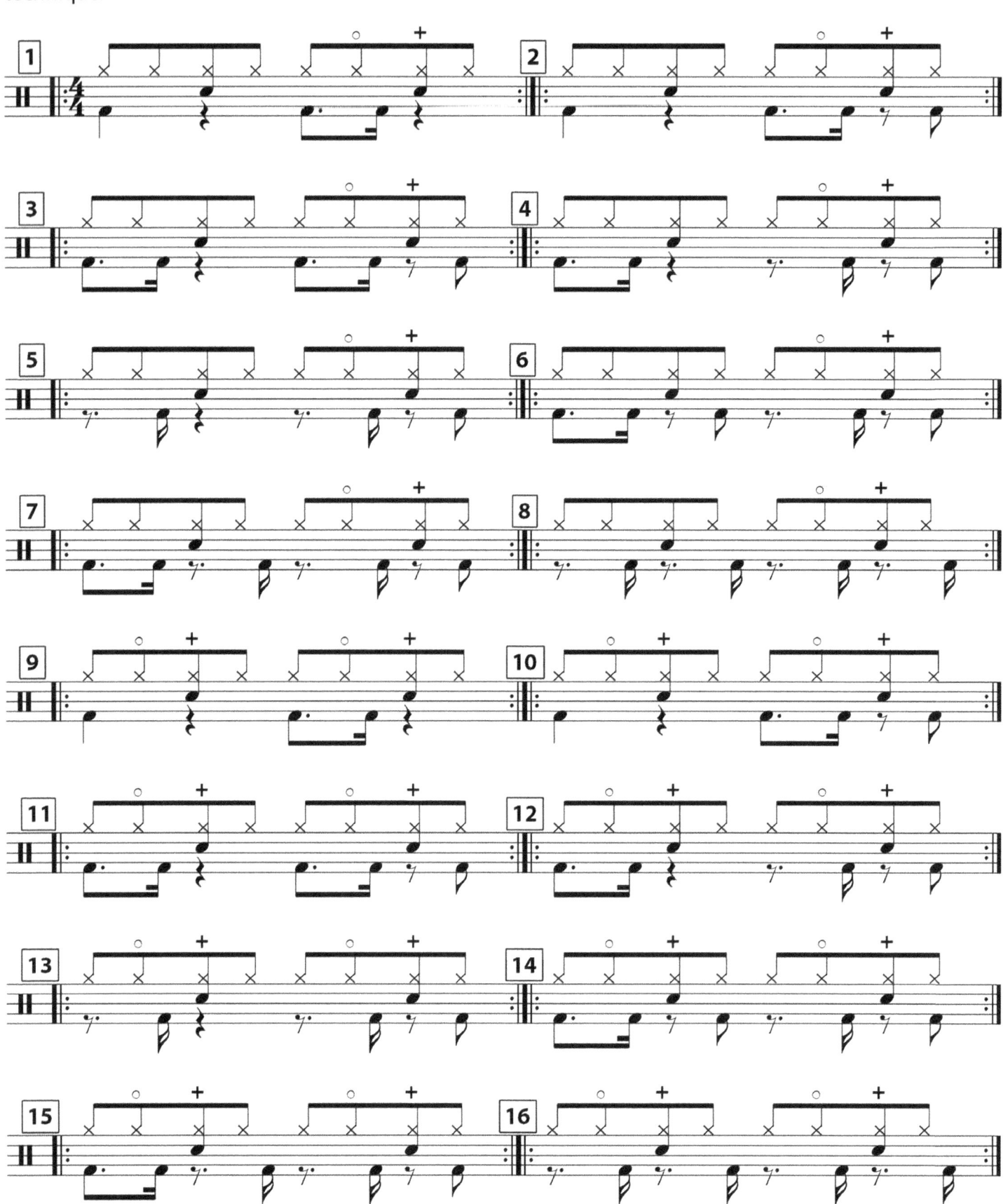

COORDINATION BUILDING (cont.)

LESSON 6 — EMBELLISHING

These exercises incorporate sixteenth-note phrasing on both the bass and snare drum along with the open hi-hat technique.

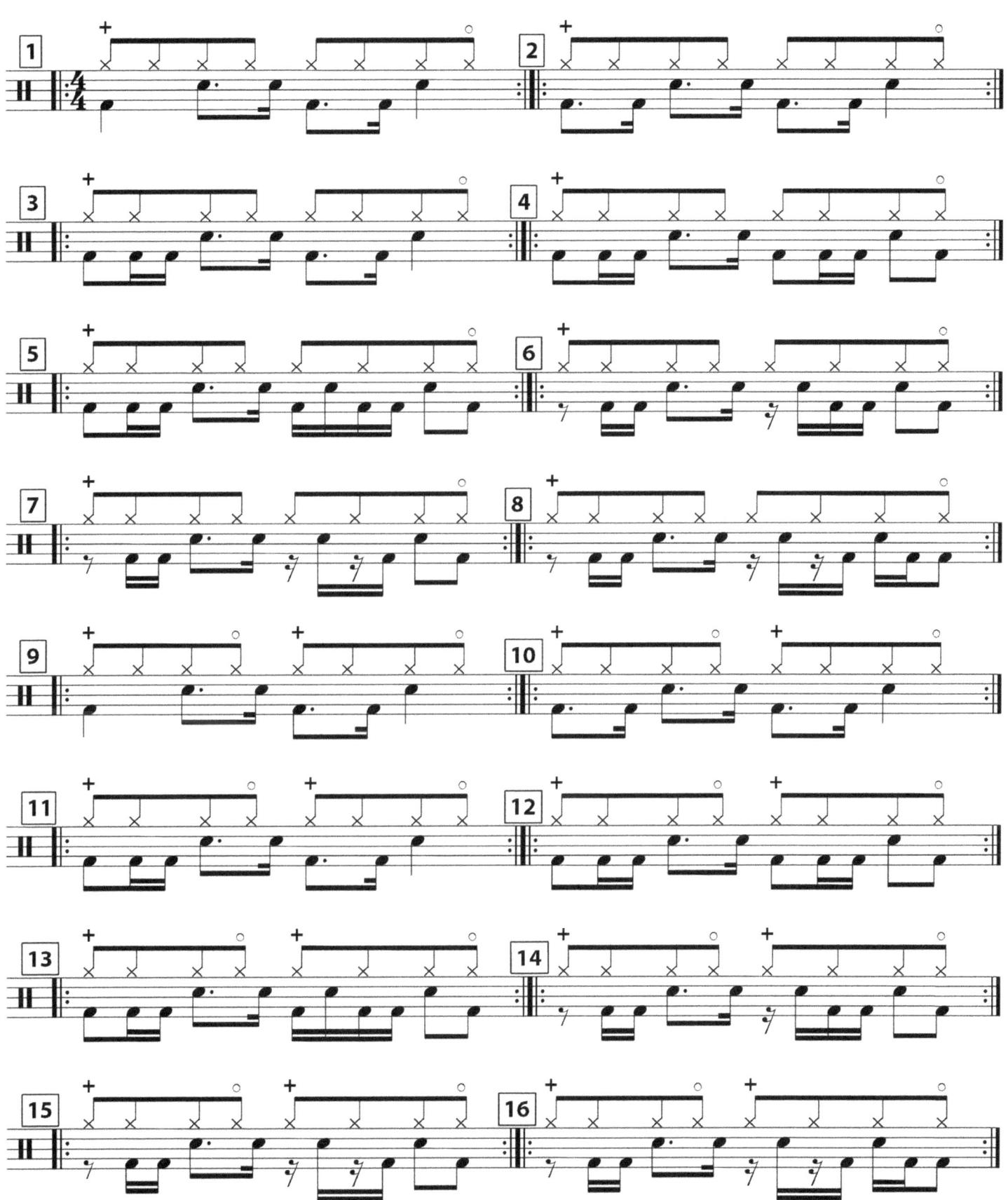

Chart-Topping Drum Beats 1 – *The 60s Through Today*

COORDINATION BUILDING (cont.)

LESSON 6 — EMBELLISHING

This page focuses on the popular disco open hi-hat pattern. You will find this pattern throughout many other styles of music, as well.

COORDINATION BUILDING (cont.)

LESSON 6 — EMBELLISHING

This section focuses on ghost-stroke coordination. Many drummers have a difficult time at first when learning to play ghost strokes. These exercises help build the muscle memory you need for ghosting.

Chart-Topping Drum Beats 1 – *The 60s Through Today*

COORDINATION BUILDING (cont.)

LESSON 6 — EMBELLISHING

Chart-Topping Drum Beats 1 – *The 60s Through Today*

COORDINATION BUILDING (cont.)

LESSON 6 — EMBELLISHING

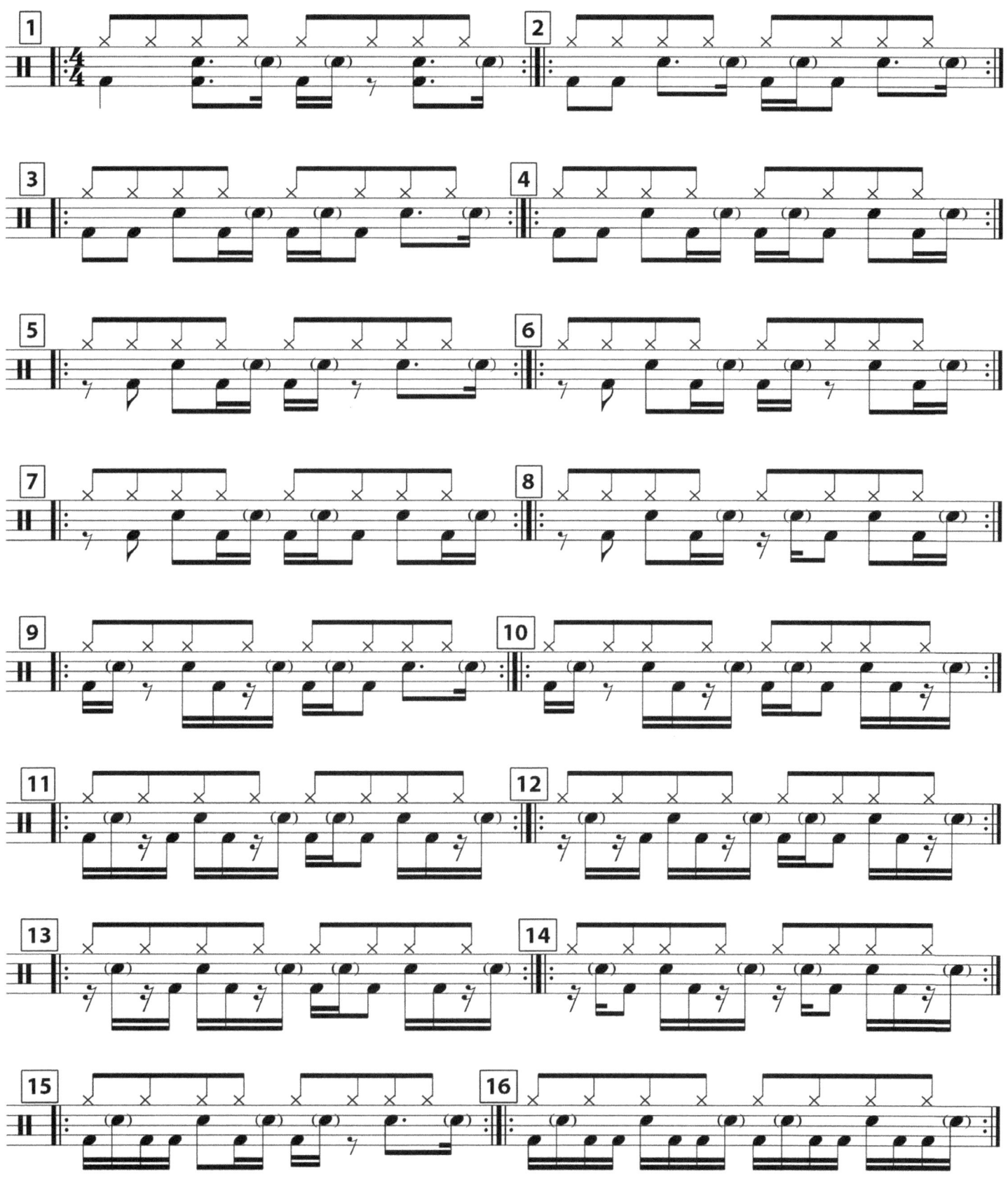

Chart-Topping Drum Beats 1 – *The 60s Through Today*

COORDINATION BUILDING (cont.)

LESSON 6 — EMBELLISHING

This final coordination building page includes both open hi-hat and ghost-stroke embellishments. These two-measure repeating grooves also pull concepts from the previous lessons.

Chart-Topping Drum Beats 1 – *The 60s Through Today*

LESSON 6

CHART-TOPPERS

EMBELLISHING

The following grooves from chart-topping songs are one-measure repeating beats that include the embellishments of the open hi-hat and/or the ghost stroke. Some of these examples include hi-hat and ghost patterns that you haven't practiced yet. Take these slowly at first, and play them until you feel comfortable with them.

Along with playing these beats, it's important to listen to the songs to get an idea of the feel these embellishments bring to the song.

I Will Buy You A New Life (verse)
Everclear (1997)

Roll To Me (Verse)
Del Amitri (1995)

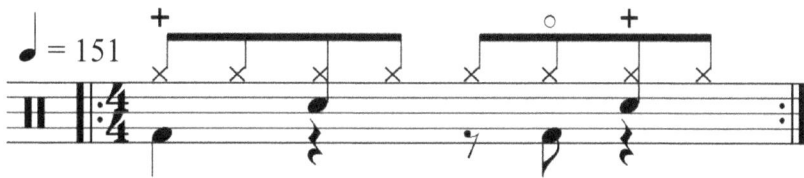

Train Train (Verse)
Blackfoot (1979)

Walk This Way (intro)
Aerosmith (1975)

Chart-Topping Drum Beats 1 – *The 60s Through Today*

LESSON 6

CHART-TOPPERS (cont.)

EMBELLISHING

Sweet Emotion (1st verse)
Aerosmith (1975)

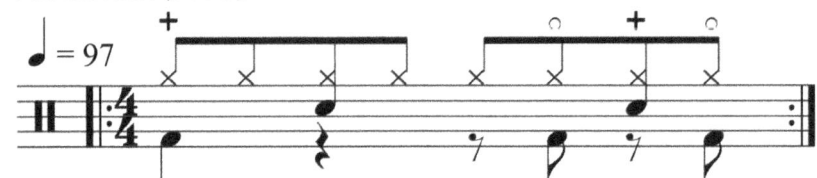

Steady As She Goes (verse)
The Raconteurs (2006)

Closing Time (2nd verse)
Semisonic (1998)

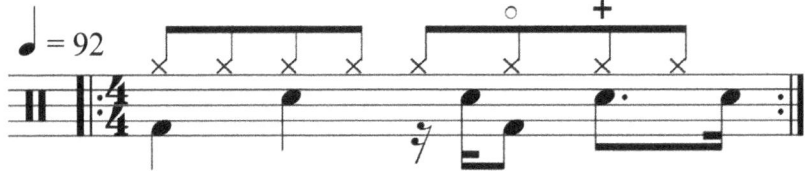

Killing In The Name (intro)
Rage Against The Machine (1992)

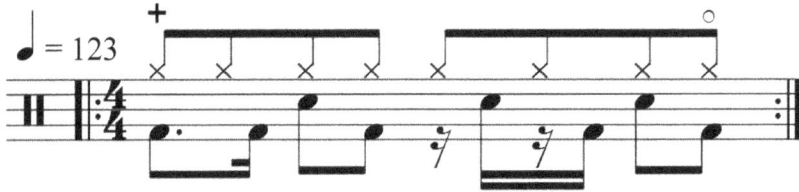

Cannonball (verse)
The Breeders (1993)

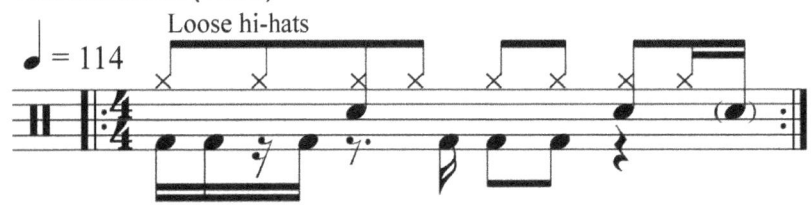

Chart-Topping Drum Beats 1 – *The 60s Through Today*

CHART-TOPPERS (cont.)

LESSON 6 — EMBELLISHING

Interstate Love Song (verse)
Stone Temple Pilots (1994)

Bombtrack (verse)
Rage Against The Machine (1993)

The World I Know (verse)
Collective Soul (1995)

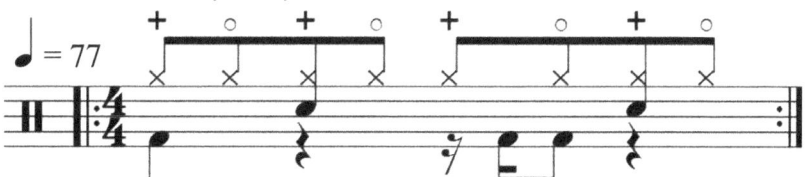

Everything I Own (chorus)
Bread (1972)

One Week (chorus)
Bare Naked Ladies (1998)

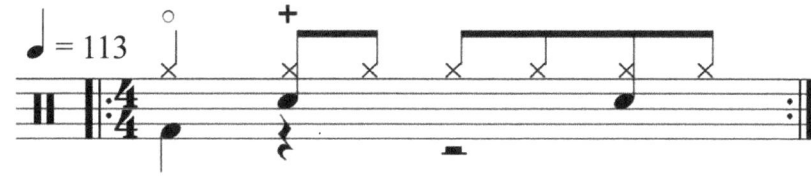

Chart-Topping Drum Beats 1 – *The 60s Through Today*

LESSON 6

CHART-TOPPERS (cont.)

EMBELLISHING

This section includes examples of multiple-measure repeating beats from chart-topping songs that include the embellishments of the open hi-hat and/or the ghost stroke.

Some of the open hi-hat and ghost stroke patterns are different than you've practiced. Take these slowly at first, playing with consistent time and increasing your speed as you become comfortable.

Stayin' Alive (verse & chorus)
Bee Gees (1977)

Smells Like Teen Spirit (verse)
Nirvana (1991)

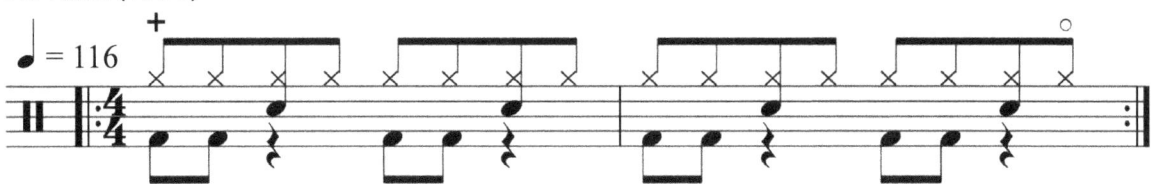

Saturday's Alright For Fighting (verse)
Elton John (1973)

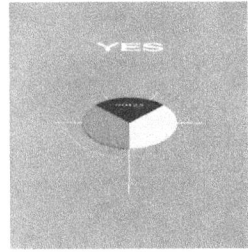

Owner Of A Lonely Heart (verse & chorus)
Yes (1983)

Chart-Topping Drum Beats 1 – *The 60s Through Today*

CHART-TOPPERS (cont.)

LESSON 6 — EMBELLISHING

The example from *Heroes*—David Bowie uses a **measure-repeat sign**. This means to repeat the previous measure. You'll see this symbol often in sheet music to save space.

Under The Bridge (chorus)
Red Hot Chili Peppers (1992)

Heart Of Glass (verse)
Blondie (1979)

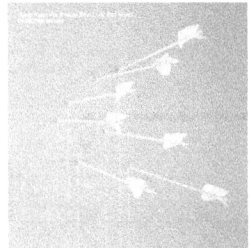

Float On (verse)
Modest Mouse (2004)

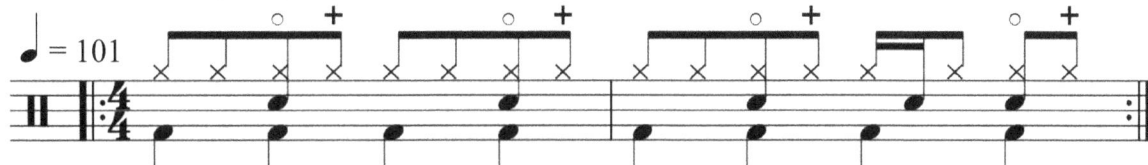

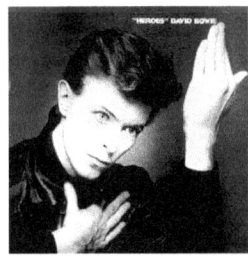

Heroes (1st verse)
David Bowie (1977)

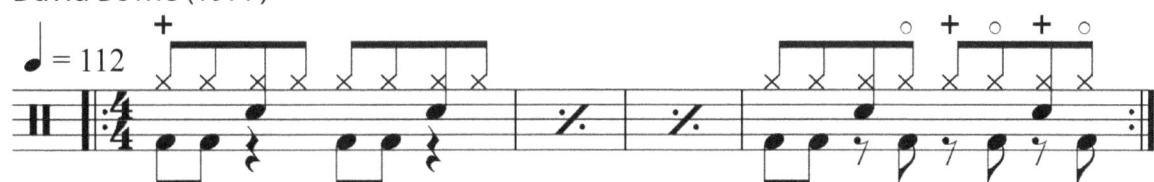

Dancing Queen (intro & chorus)
ABBA (1976)

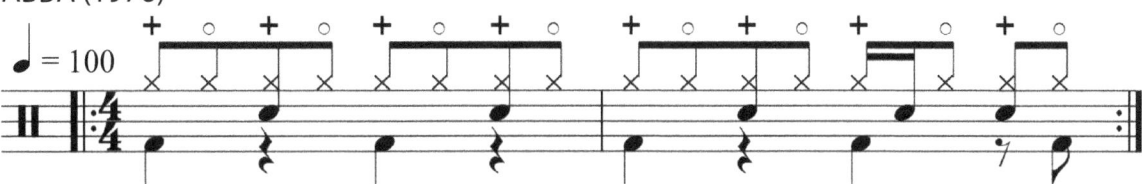

Chart-Topping Drum Beats 1 – *The 60s Through Today*

CHART-TOPPERS (cont.)

LESSON 6 — EMBELLISHING

I Sat By The Ocean (verse)
Queens Of The Stoneage (2013)

Brick House (chorus)
Commodores (1977)

Long Train Running (intro & 1st verse)
Doobie Brothers (1973)

Revolution Earth (verse)
B-52's (1992)
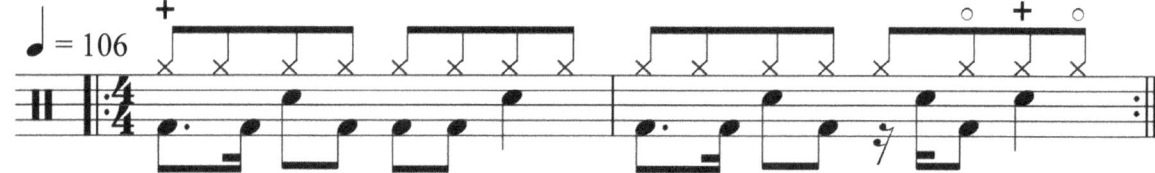

We Are Family (chorus)
Sister Sledge (1979)
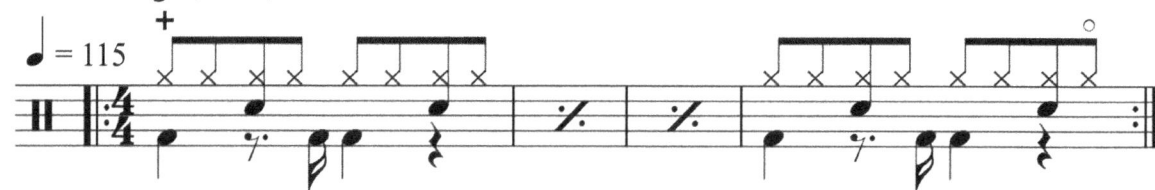

Chart-Topping Drum Beats 1 – *The 60s Through Today*

CHART-TOPPERS (cont.)

LESSON 6 — EMBELLISHING

Sweet Home Alabama (intro & re-intro)
Lynyrd Skynryd (1974)

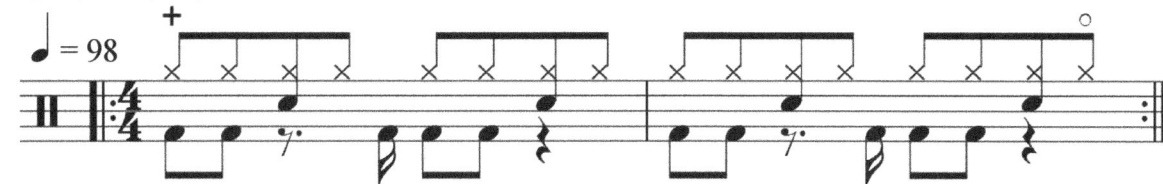

This Love (verse)
Maroon 5 (2004)

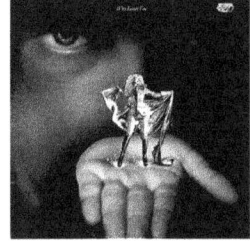

December, 1963 (Oh, What A Night) (verse & chorus)
The Four Seasons (1975)

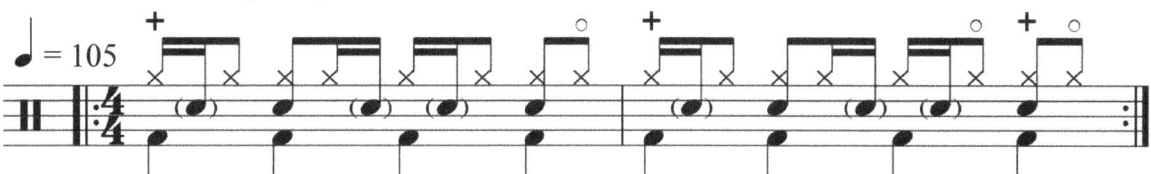

Save Tonight (verse)
Eagle Eye Cherry (1997)

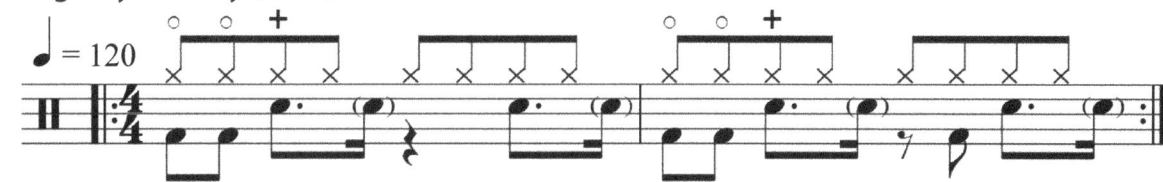

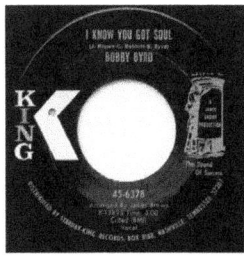

I Know You Got Soul (verse & chorus)
Bobby Byrd & James Brown (1971)

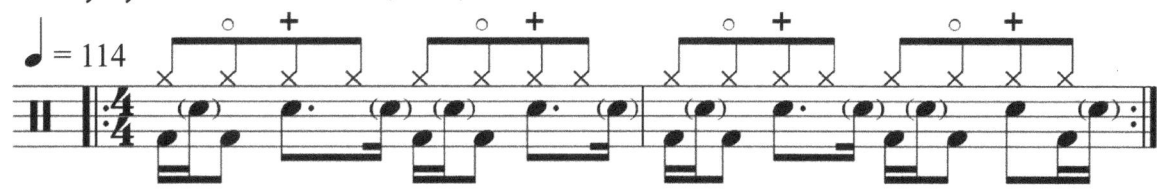

Chart-Topping Drum Beats 1 – The 60s Through Today

COMPOSITION

LESSON 6

EMBELLISHING

Continue developing your own unique embellishing style by adding ghost strokes and open hi-hats to the rhythms below. Remember to take your time with this to make sure each rhythm nails your tastes.

PART A
DIRECTIONS: Write open hi-hats to the rhythms below to embellish the grooves.

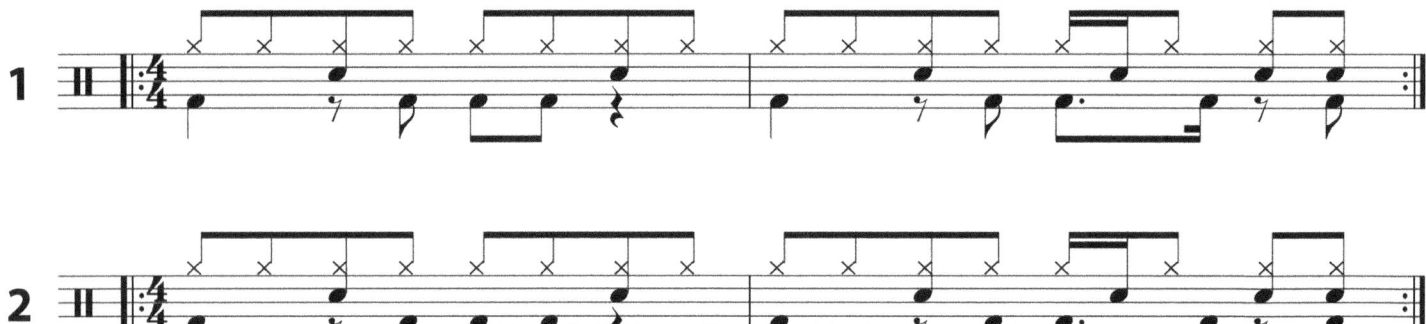

PART B
DIRECTIONS: Add ghost strokes to the rhythms below to embellish the grooves.

PART C
DIRECTIONS: Write both ghost strokes and open hi-hats to the rhythms below to embellish the grooves.

OUR OTHER PRINT PUBLICATIONS

Chart-Topping Drum Fills
The 60s Through Today

onlinedrummer.com/chart-topping-drum-fills/

by Dawn Richardson

COORDINATION BUILDING EBOOKS

... AND MORE!

onlinedrummer.com/category/ebooks/